CASUAL
DINING

ALLYSON GOFTON

CORBANS GOOD FOOD & WINE
SERIES

WITH  MAGAZINE

David Bateman

Dedication

To Warwick, who shares my love of food, wine, entertaining and good times with friends and family.

Credits

Grateful thanks to the following who kindly loaned props for the photography of this book:
Jane at Trumps of Remuera; Jocelyn and team at The Studio of Tableware, Mt Eden; and Margaux,
Julie and team at Corso Di Fiori, Newmarket, and Robyn and her team at Indigo.
A special thanks to *Next* magazine, who have allowed many of their photographs, including
some by Nick Tresidder and Mike Stephen, to be reprinted in this book.

Published in 1995 by David Bateman Ltd, Tarndale Grove, Albany Business Park, Bush Road, Albany,
North Shore City, Auckland, New Zealand

ISBN 1 86953 196 5

Photographs by Alan Gillard
Printed in Hong Kong by Colorcraft Ltd

Introduction

The word 'dining' conjures up visions of exquisite and expensive table settings complemented by fabulous food that is difficult to prepare. This is not the case today. Dining is about good food, which may take a little longer to prepare but can be simply enjoyed without too much work, with good company, great wine and a touch more finesse than we had in *Casual Eating*.

Casual dining should still be hassle-free, but I do take a little more trouble. There are plenty of reasons to go a little bit further for friends and family and this book has a delightful collection of foods to enjoy on such occasions. I hope *Casual Dining* will inspire you to find a reason to enjoy a casual dinner party with friends and family. In a world that seems to be constantly 'time poor', we must make time to be with them, and although such occasions require a bit of organisation they also provide plenty of fun.

My grateful thanks to the team of people who helped with *Casual Dining*: the wine team, who selected the wines to match our menus (such a hard job, but we had to do it!) – Noel Scanlan, Martin Carrington and Sue Rickerby (from Corbans Wines); Glenda Neil (wine writer and colleague from *Next* Magazine); and Ron Small (wine judge and columnist); Lindsey Dawson, my editor at *Next*, and her staff, who constantly give me inspiration; to super colleagues Ann Boardman and Pauline Willoughby for their support and back up when time ran short; photographer and friend Alan Gillard for his fabulous photos; and the writing team, Tracey Borgfeldt and Ann Clifford, my editors, who wait patiently for my copy and give much encouragement along the way. And last, because he is probably the most important, my husband Warwick; who gives me all his spare time and more to help and allows me to ruin his waistline further.

This book should be the beginning of many fun dinner parties, '90s style. So find an excuse to celebrate, get your friends together and have a good time. Remember the dishes can always be done the next day, so enjoy!

Contents

Pan Fried Fish in Lemon Curry

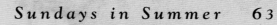

Pasta with Courgettes & Pinenuts

Peaches in Merlot & Vanilla

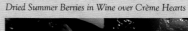

Dried Summer Berries in Wine over Crème Hearts

Peach & Pecan Upsidedown Cake

Lamb Rump with Fresh Herbs

Turkey & Berry Salad

Roast Chicken with Lavendar & Basil

The Wine Cellar Guide

If you would like to begin a wine cellar, here's a guide from our team on what you need to get started.

Six bottles each of:

* High quality French Champagne, such as Taittinger, for special celebrations and gift giving.

* Good NZ Méthode Champenoise, such as Amadeus, for brunches and celebrations.

* Slightly lower-priced Chardonnay, such as Corbans Estate Gisborne, for good value drinking.

* Premium brand barrel-fermented Chardonnay, such as Corbans Private Bin Gisborne Chardonnay, for those bold seafood and white meat dishes.

* Young aggressive Sauvignon Blanc such as the classic Stoneleigh Vineyard Marlborough for all those who love wine that is best enjoyed without food.

* Oaked Sauvignon Blanc (possibly labelled Fumé Blanc) for vegetarian and other herb influenced dishes.

* Full-bodied Gewurztraminer such as Longridge of Hawkes Bay. A wine type which is vastly underrated in NZ and capable of aging extremely well. Gewurztraminer is ideal with spicy Thai and Indian foods.

* Dry Riesling such as Corbans Private Bin Amberley Rhine Riesling. Riesling has good natural acids and also tends to age extremely well. It can accompany spicy dishes but is also excellent with poultry in fruit sauces. Riesling suits a wide range of palates and tastes.

* Dessert wine, such as an extremely good botrytised Riesling. This is always a great finale to a good dinner; try it with a mature blue cheese or, for something different, as a starter with a rich pâté.

* Pinot Noir for those classic game dishes.

* Hearty Cabernet Sauvignon or Cabernet Sauvignon Merlot for barbeques and traditional roasts or casseroles.

* Light fruity red, such as a Beaujolais, ideal served chilled at picnics.

Mid-week Dining

Dining mid-week means there's usually less time to be spent on preparation: a quick visit to the supermarket or fresh vege man on the way home with maybe half an hour to spare if you are lucky. These ideas are quick and simple, ideal for that casual dinner after work. Enjoy them with a good bottle of wine and finish with a fruit dessert or a platter of cheese and crackers.

Herbed Ham & Courgette Frittata

1 tblsp oil
1 onion, peeled and diced
1 clove garlic, peeled and diced
500 grams courgettes, trimmed and thickly sliced
125 grams shredded ham
3 eggs
2 tblsp chopped fresh herbs (thyme, marjoram or parsley)
2 tblsp toasted pinenuts
4 dried tomatoes in oil, finely sliced

1 Heat the oil in a non-stick frying pan about 20 cm in diameter and add the onion and garlic. Cook for 1-2 minutes until fragrant.

2 Add the courgettes and ham. Toss over the heat for about 5-8 minutes, until the courgettes become slightly golden and the onions are cooked. Spread out evenly in the pan.

3 Beat the eggs together with a good shake of salt and pepper. Add the herbs and pour into the pan. Cook over a moderate heat for about 3 minutes until the egg has set.

4 Serve cut into wedges. Garnish with the pinenuts and dried tomatoes. Serve with a fresh salad and crusty bread.

Serves 4

Wine Selection

A light meal with lots of herbal vegetable flavours. Try a current vintage Sauvignon Blanc that is crisp and dry. Our wine suggestion: Longridge of Hawkes Bay Oak Aged Sauvignon Blanc or Corbans Estate Gisborne Sauvignon Blanc.

Fish Basquaise

Fresh fish cooked simply with the flavours of peppers, tomatoes and olives. Just delicious if you are an olive lover.

1 clove garlic, peeled and crushed
3 tblsp lemon juice
4 tblsp olive oil
750 grams thick white fish fillets, diced into 2-cm pieces
1 green and 1 red pepper
1 onion, peeled and diced
2 tblsp tomato paste

400 gram can chopped tomatoes in juice
1 tblsp freshly chopped oregano
½ cup green olives
freshly ground black pepper
1-2 tsp fresh oregano leaves for garnish

1 Combine the garlic, lemon juice and 3 tblsp of the olive oil together. Toss over the fish and leave for at least 30 minutes.

2 Grill the red and green peppers under a hot grill until the skins are charred and blistered. Put them in a plastic bag, seal loosely and allow to cool for about 10 minutes. Skin under cool running water. Core, deseed and cut the peppers into 2-cm pieces.

3 Gently pan fry the onion in the remaining measure of olive oil until soft but not brown. Stir in tomato paste and cook, stirring constantly, for 4-5 minutes until it begins to darken in colour. Add tomatoes in juice and stir well.

4 Drain fish and discard marinade. Carefully fold fish pieces into hot sauce and simmer very gently for about 5 minutes.

5 Add chopped oregano, olives and roasted peppers to the pan and season with ground pepper. Simmer for about 5 minutes or until the fish is cooked.

6 Garnish with fresh oregano leaves and serve with rice, pasta or chunks of fresh bread. A fresh green bean salad would be an ideal partner for this dish.

Serves 5-6

Wine Selection

Sauvignon Blanc and tomatoes are a great combination. The acid in the wine and the fruit seem to work well togther to reduce the effect in both. Our wine suggestion: Corbans Private Bin Sauvignon Blanc or Stoneleigh Sauvignon Blanc.

Olives

Whoever transformed olives from the incredibly bitter fruit into the delicacy we know today was a genius. Olives come in different colours that reflect the degree of ripeness. Some, like the Manzanilla from Spain, are best eaten green, while the ebony Kalamata olives from Greece are better fully ripe. The main varieties available are:

Manzanilla Available either plain or stuffed. Use unstoned olives for marinating or cooking. Stuffed olives are ideal for an antipasto platter.

Kalamata My favourite. These are perfect for eating or for adding to salads or stews.

Mission Olives From Spain or Greece, these are the round fat olives that fall away easily from the stone, making them best for stoning and purÇeing or making into tapenade.

Niçoise Olives Hailing from Italy and France (the Mediterranean area), these small black olives are best for salads and marinating.

Dried Olives Wonderfully full of flavour. They are first packed in salt to draw out all their moisture before being marinated in herbed oils or brines. Use as part of an antipasto.

Tasteless olives are never a lost cause; if you have bought some that you are unhappy with marinate them.

2 cups black and green olives
2 lemons
2 fresh red chillies, deseeded and sliced
2 cloves garlic, peeled and finely sliced
2 tblsp chopped fresh herbs (marjoram, thyme, oregano and parsley)
about ¾ cup olive oil

1 Hold 5 to 6 olives together on a board and lightly bruise with a wooden rolling pin. Do not crush.

2 Pare the rind off the lemons using a zester.

3 In a bowl, combine olives, lemon strips, chillies, garlic and herbs. Put into a container with a cover.

4 Pour over enough olive oil to cover the olives, cover the container and marinate for at least 24 hours. The olives will keep well for up to 3 weeks in a very cool place. *If your kitchen is warm keep them in the fridge.*

5 Drain to serve. Use reserved oil to cook with. Serve with drinks, and be prepared to become addicted to olives after you have sampled these!

Dijon Scotch Fillet

Roasting a piece of meat may sound time-consuming, but this topping is quickly prepared and the meat can be in the oven when guests arrive.

2 cloves garlic, peeled and mashed
3 tblsp wholeseed mustard
1 kg piece Scotch fillet steak
6 rashers bacon

1 Blend together the garlic and wholeseed mustard and spread it thickly over the top of the Scotch fillet, spreading it down the sides.

2 Trim rind off bacon and arrange on top. Secure with a piece of string if necessary.

3 Place the meat on a rack in a roasting dish and cook at 180°C for 1 hour.

I also cook by temperature probe to about 64°C, however the temperature degree most suitable for you may vary according to your oven so you may need to practise this.

4 Remove the meat from the oven and cover with foil. Allow it to stand for 10 minutes before carving. Serve sliced, hot or cold, with a fresh green salad and potatoes or pasta.

Serves 6

Wine Selection

Loads of flavours in this dish call for a robust rich red wine. Try a Cabernet/Merlot with lots of ripe fruit and oak. Our wine suggestion: Corbans Private Bin Hawkes Bay Cabernet Sauvignon or Longridge of Hawkes Bay Cabernet/Merlot.

Cook's Tip

If you have a probe selection in your oven but have never used it, do try it. Cooking by probe is great once you have the hang of it and your meat will turn out perfectly every time. These temperatures are a guide to cook by and should be varied to suit your own taste:

- *60°C will give you rare meat (I prefer to cook to 64°C).*
- *70°C will give you medium pink.*
- *80°C will give you well-done meat.*

Grilled Rosemary & Sage Lamb Chops

Spring lamb chops cooked until pink and flavoured with rosemary and sage and a good squeeze of lemon juice just before serving are quick and delicious.

2 tblsp rosemary leaves
about 4 small sage leaves
¼ cup good quality virgin olive oil
grated rind and juice of 1 juicy lemon
6-8 lamb loin chops or 4 lamb steaks

1 Crush the rosemary and sage leaves with your hands and place in a shallow dish with olive oil, lemon rind and juice.

2 Place the lamb chops or steaks in the marinade and season well with pepper. Marinate for 30 minutes.

3 Heat the grill or a frying pan until very hot and cook the lamb quickly on both sides to your taste. Allow 5-6 minutes per side for steaks.

Serves 4

Roasted Summer Vegetables

Slice summer vegetables, such as courgettes and aubergines, into thick slices. Trim spring onions and beans, and halve tomatoes and mushrooms. Place the vegetables on a foil-lined tray and brush liberally with olive oil. Grill under a high heat until the vegetables are slightly blackened, then turn and do the other side. Season well with salt and pepper and sprinkle with fresh herbs like parsley and rosemary.

Wine Selection

A light fruity red wine will go well with the flavours of both the lamb and the roasted vegetables. Our wine suggestion: Stoneleigh Vineyard Marlborough Cabernet Sauvignon or Robard & Butler Shiraz.

Pan Fried Fish in Lemon Curry

Delicious with John Dory or orange roughy fillets.

75 grams butter

1 tsp turmeric

1 tsp ground cumin

2 cloves garlic, peeled and chopped

2 stalks lemon grass, trimmed and sliced

2-3 spring onions, trimmed and finely chopped

4 fresh fillets fish (skinned and boned)

1 punnet cherry tomatoes, halved

about 2 tblsp chopped fresh parsley

1 Heat the butter in a frying pan and add the turmeric, cumin, garlic, lemon grass and spring onion. Cook over a low heat for about 4-5 minutes until quite fragrant but the spices or butter have not begun to burn.

2 Increase the heat, pushing the contents of the pan to the side, and add the fish fillets. Cook over a moderate heat for about 3 minutes on each side until the fish is about halfway to being cooked.

3 Add the tomatoes and parsley and season well with salt and pepper. Allow the tomatoes to soften and then serve.

This is wonderful with creamy mashed potatoes!

Serves 4

Wine Selection

Choose a Riesling with lots of limey fruit to complement the lemon and spice of this dish. Our wine suggestion: the classic Stoneleigh Vineyard Marlborough Riesling.

Cook's Tip

When cooking with spices it is always best to cook them in butter or oil first to release their essential oils. If you add them as they are to a dish, they never really lose their raw taste. Remember to use only the bottom white part of the lemon grass (about 3 cm). The remainder of the stalk is stringy and can be used for flavouring stocks.

Asian Chicken Livers on Salad Greens

Chicken livers pan-fried with wonderful herbs and flavourings make a quick and economical meal. Serve with a selection of lettuces and other salad greens.

400 grams chicken livers
1 tsp freshly ground black or white pepper
2 tblsp dry sherry
2 tblsp clarified butter or olive oil
2 cloves garlic, peeled and crushed
1 tblsp finely chopped fresh ginger
2 spring onions, trimmed and sliced
1 fresh red chilli, deseeded and sliced
230 gram can water chestnuts, well drained and sliced
salad leaves for 4, washed and crispy
fresh chopped coriander

Dressing

1 tblsp light soy sauce
2 tblsp peanut oil
drop or two of sesame oil
1 tblsp lemon juice
1 tsp honey
¼ tsp sambal oelek or chilli powder

1 Trim the chicken livers and slice into 2 or 3 pieces. Season with pepper and sherry and set aside for 2 minutes.

2 Heat the butter or oil in a frying pan and add the garlic, ginger, spring onions and chilli. Toss over a moderately high heat for about 3-4 minutes until quite fragrant. Set aside.

3 Re-heat the pan and add the livers. Toss over a moderately high heat. Once they are sealed, return the vegetables to the pan and add the water chestnuts.

4 Allow the livers to cook over a lower heat for a few minutes until they are pink, or a little more well done, depending on your taste.

5 Once cooked, remove from the heat. Arrange the salad leaves on a large platter and toss through the dressing and livers.

6 Serve warm, garnished with fresh chopped coriander.

For the dressing, put all ingredients into a jar and shake vigorously to blend.

Serves 4

Wine Selection

Asian spices and Gewurztraminer are always good together, but a dry Riesling will work just as well with this meal. Our wine suggestion: Corbans Estate Marlborough Gewurztraminer or Corbans Private Bin Amberley Riesling.

Seared Chicken Couscous Salad

It is very easy to be creative with chicken breasts. Served here with couscous, which takes next to no time to prepare, you have a super quick meal.

2 double chicken breasts
freshly ground black pepper
1 tsp ground paprika
2 tblsp olive oil

1 Rub the chicken breasts well with the pepper, paprika and olive oil. You can remove the skin if you wish.

2 Heat a frying pan and pan-fry the chicken breasts until tender. Alternatively bake at 180°C for about 35-40 minutes on a rack in or until cooked. Keep warm.

Couscous Salad

1½ cups couscous
1½ cups chicken stock
1 red pepper, grilled, peeled, deseeded and diced
3-4 spring onions
2 cloves garlic, peeled and crushed
2 oranges, peeled and segmented
2 tblsp chopped fresh thyme or basil (optional)
½ cup chopped fresh parsley
1 tblsp wholeseed mustard
½ cup vinaigrette (see page 78)

1 Place the couscous in a bowl and pour over the chicken stock. Set aside for about 10 minutes until the couscous has absorbed all the liquid.

2 Fluff up and toss through an extra tablespoon of olive oil.

3 In a large bowl toss the couscous, red pepper, spring onions, garlic, orange pieces, thyme or basil, parsley, wholeseed mustard and vinaigrette. Season well with salt and pepper.

4 Serve the chicken breast sliced beside the couscous on a large dinner plate.

Serves 4

Variation

Use fillets of lamb and add a little chopped mint to the couscous.

Wine Selection

You could match the flavours of the peppers, onions and herbs with a Sauvignon Blanc, or, for a good contrast, try a light Chardonnay without too much oak. Our wine suggestion: Stoneleigh Vineyard Marlborough Sauvignon Blanc or Corbans Estate Gisborne Chardonnay.

Strawberry & Grand Marnier Compôte

Take fresh strawberries and poach them gently in an orange liqueur for a lovely light dessert that takes very little time to prepare.

1 kg strawberries, wiped and hulled
¼ cup Grand Marnier (orange liqueur)
¾ cup water
½ cup sugar
1 tsp grated orange rind
½ cup orange juice

1 Divide the strawberries into two equal piles, keeping the best-looking smaller strawberries in one pile. Place these in a bowl with the Grand Marnier and set aside to soften. Cut the remaining strawberries in half.

2 Put the water, sugar, orange rind and orange juice in a saucepan and bring to the boil. Add the halved strawberries and poach gently for 10 minutes, or until the berries are quite tender.

3 Put the poached berries into a food processor and process until smooth. Allow to cool.

4 Combine the puréed and whole berries in a bowl and allow to stand for 1 hour before serving.

Serves 6

Cook's Tip

These are best served cool, but not ice-cold, from the fridge.

Ginger Baked Pears

Baked fruits are such a simple dessert; there is hardly any preparation and once in the oven there is absolutely nothing to do.

4 firm pears that are not too under-ripe
½ cup dessert wine
½ cup water
¼ cup caster sugar
2-3 cm piece fresh ginger, peeled
½ cup cream or double cream

1 Peel the pears and cut a small piece from the base so that they stand upright. Place them in a small but deep ovenproof dish.

2 In a saucepan bring the dessert wine, water, caster sugar and ginger to the boil, then pour over the pears.

3 Bake at 180°C for about 50 minutes or until a skewer can be inserted without any resistance. Transfer the pears to a heatproof serving dish.

4 Put the cooking juices into a saucepan and add the cream. Boil rapidly for 4 minutes until the mixture has reduced by about a quarter. Discard the piece of ginger. Pour over the pears to serve. Serve hot or cold.

Serves 4

Wine Selection

Match this dessert with any sweet wine style. Our wine suggestion: Corbans Private Bin Late Harvest Semillon Sauvignon Blanc.

Great Occasions

A celebration of any kind is always a good reason to expend a little more effort. Whether it be a family reunion, a special birthday, engagement or Christmas, sharing a home-cooked meal with good wine, plenty of laughter and talk makes for great memories. Food should be elegant, without *too* much trouble in preparation. Many of these menus can be mixed and matched to suit, the key is to have a great time.

M e n u

Scallop Mousse with Saffron Hollandaise

Turkey with Hazelnuts and Grapes

Chocolate Liqueur Torte

  ✐ ✐ ✐ ✐ ✐

Scallop Mousse with Saffron Hollandaise

This is a very special dish for a dinner party. It can be served as a main course with vegetables or simply as an entrée.

250 grams scallops
250 grams firm white fish fillets (such as snapper),
  cut into large pieces
2 egg whites
2 cups cream
1 tsp salt
white pepper
2 courgettes

Saffron Hollandaise

¼ tsp saffron threads
3 tblsp white wine vinegar
6 whole peppercorns
2 egg yolks
125 grams unsalted butter

1 Remove the roes from the scallops. Put fish pieces and scallops in a food processor and process until they form a paste.

2 With the motor running, gradually incorporate the egg whites. Once the egg whites are added, gradually pour in the cream. *Make sure that the mixture does not get warm. If it does, put the mixture in the fridge for 30 minutes before continuing.* Season well with salt and white pepper.

3 Trim the ends from the courgettes and peel them lengthwise into thin strips. Blanch the strips in boiling water, refresh quickly in cold and dry well on paper towels. Use to line the base and sides of 8 greased half-cup capacity moulds.

4 Fill each mould halfway with mousse and then arrange the scallop roes evenly on top. Cover with remaining mousse. Cover each mould with greased foil. Place in a *bain marie* (water bath) and cook at 180°C for 20 minutes or until just firm to the touch.

5 Turn the moulds out onto a plate and serve with Saffron Hollandaise.

S e r v e s   8

Saffron Hollandaise

1 Put the saffron, vinegar and peppercorns into a saucepan and simmer for 5 minutes. There should be 1 tblsp of vinegar remaining. Allow the saffron to infuse for 10 minutes.

2 Remove the peppercorns from the vinegar and add the vinegar to the egg yolks in the top of a double boiler. Whisk over simmering water until the egg yolks are light.

3 Add knobs of butter, about 1 tablespoon at a time, and whisk into the eggs until the mixture is thick and creamy. Season as wished.

W i n e   S e l e c t i o n

This rich creamy dish should be matched with a young Chardonnay. Choose one that is big and buttery with a good acid backbone. Our Wine Suggestion: Corbans Private Bin Gisborne Chardonnay or Cooks Winemakers Reserve Chardonnay.

Turkey with Hazelnuts & Grapes

If you're looking for something different for your festive Christmas or mid-winter Christmas dinner, try this easy idea.

1 turkey buffet breast, well defrosted
juice of 1 lemon

2 tblsp olive oil
salt and pepper to season

Stuffing

70-gram packet of hazelnuts, toasted
2 rashers bacon, trimmed and sliced finely
4 slices wholemeal toast bread, crumbed
25 grams butter

½ tsp salt
grated rind of 1 lemon
1 tsp sugar
pepper
1 egg
¼ cup water

Sauce

50 grams butter
4 shallots, peeled and diced (or 2 tblsp minced onion)
¼ cup port

2 cups chicken stock
1 strip lemon rind
2 tblsp flour
2 cups sliced grapes

1 Using a sharp knife, cut the breast from the bone. Use the bones for making stock. Trim away the wing portions and add them to the stock pot. Using your fingers, carefully pull back the skin from the top of the turkey, keeping the skin intact.

2 Mix lemon juice with the olive oil and salt and pepper. Rub into the turkey breast meat. Pull the turkey skin back over the breasts and refrigerate for 1 hour while preparing the stuffing.

3 Press the stuffing mixture between the skin and breast meat. Pull the skin back over to cover the stuffing. Secure the skin firmly in place with a few toothpicks.

4 Transfer the turkey to a roasting tray and brush lightly with olive oil. Roast at 180°C for 1-1¼ hours until the turkey is tender.

5 Allow to stand 10 minutes before carving and serving with the grape sauce.

Serves 8

Stuffing

1 Rub the skins from the toasted hazelnuts.

2 Cook the bacon in a lightly oiled sauté pan until crisp.

3 Transfer to a food processor with the hazelnuts, breadcrumbs, butter, grated lemon rind, salt, sugar and pepper and process for 1-2 minutes. Pulse in the egg and water.

Sauce

1 Melt half the butter in a frying pan, add the shallots and cook over a low heat for 10-15 minutes until softened.

2 Add the port and allow the mixture to simmer until all the port has evaporated.

3 Stir in the chicken stock and lemon strip and allow to simmer for 5 minutes.

4 Blend the remaining butter and the flour together, and stir into the pan. Add the grapes. Simmer for 2 minutes. Remove lemon strip before serving.

Cook's Tip

You can prepare the sauce in the pan the turkey was cooked in, to use all the flavours from the turkey as well. Keep the turkey covered to keep warm while preparing the sauce.

Wine Selection

Match the nutty sweet flavours here with either an elegant red wine or a well oaked Chardonnay. Our wine suggestion: For the red try the Stoneleigh Cabernet Sauvignon or the Robard & Butler Shiraz. For the Chardonnay, we recommend the Corbans Private Bin Gisborne Chardonnay.

Chocolate Liqueur Torte

This is definitely not a dieters' recipe but a special torte ideal for a festive occasion.

550 grams cooking chocolate
½ cup coffee liqueur, such as Kahlua
150-gram tub double cream
½ cup cream
2 egg whites
2 tblsp caster sugar
1½ cups crushed Amaretti biscuits

1 Break up the chocolate and place into the top of a double saucepan with the coffee liqueur. Heat over simmering water until the chocolate has melted. Remove from heat and stir in double cream. Alternatively, melt the chocolate and coffee liqueur in a microwave on medium temperature.

2 When the mixture is very cool but not set, beat the cream until thick.

3 In a clean bowl, beat the egg whites until they form stiff peaks and sprinkle in the caster sugar. Beat to a soft meringue-like mixture.

4 Fold the chocolate mixture into the cream, and then fold in the egg whites.

5 Sprinkle the crushed Amaretti biscuits onto the base of a lightly greased and paper-lined, 24-cm round loose-bottom cake tin. Pour in the chocolate torte mixture. Refrigerate overnight.

6 To serve, run a warm cloth just around the outside of the cake tin. Remove the sides of the tin and slide the torte carefully onto a serving platter.

7 Serve chilled. Accompany with fresh berry fruits marinated in a sprinkling of sugar and a little favourite liqueur.

S E R V E S   1 2 - 1 6

*Seared Poussin with Roasted Garlic &
Sun-dried Tomatoes*

Basil Spiked Pickled Sweet Red Peppers

Olive Oil & Sauterne Cake with Citrus Syllabub

✑✑✑✑✑

Seared Poussin with Roasted Garlic & Sun-dried Tomatoes

Baby chickens roasted with the flavours of garlic and sun-dried tomatoes are great for summer eating. Try the Basil Spiked Pickled Sweet Red Peppers as an accompaniment.

1 small bulb of garlic	*2 rashers bacon, trimmed*
4 poussins	*and diced*
4 tblsp sun-dried tomato	*2 tblsp flour*
paste	*plenty freshly ground black*
4 tblsp olive oil or melted	*pepper*
butter	*1 cup chicken stock*

1 Wrap the garlic bulb in foil, drizzle with a little olive oil and place in a 180°C oven for 1 hour or until a skewer can be inserted without any resistance.

2 With a sharp knife or a pair of kitchen scissors, cut down either side of the back bone of each poussin to remove it. Use the bones to make the stock. Flatten the birds by pressing down firmly on the breast.

3 Using your index finger, loosen the skin from each bird around the breast and thigh area. Spread about 1 tblsp sun-dried tomato paste under the skin and over the meat. Pull the skin firmly down over the birds. If you wish, secure the birds in position with wooden skewers.

4 Place the poussins on a rack in a roasting dish and rub over the oil or melted butter. Sprinkle evenly with the chopped bacon and sift over the flour. Season well with plenty of pepper. If you have a fan grill oven, place the birds in the lower part of the oven and fan grill at 180°C for 25-30 minutes until they are cooked. To check this, pierce between the leg joint to see if the juice is clear. If it is still pink, continue to cook. The fan grilling will give the poussins a lovely crisp golden top. If you do not have a fan grill, bake at 180°C for 30-35 minutes until cooked. Stand covered for 10 minutes while preparing the sauce.

5 Remove the garlic from the foil and cut in half horizontally. Squeeze out the cooked garlic centre into the pan and pour in the chicken stock.

6 Bring the pan to the boil and stir well to include any tasty sediment in the pan gravy. Season with salt and pepper. Skim off any fat that may come to the top.

7 Place one poussin on each plate and pour over sauce. Serve with wild rice, creamed spinach and Basil Spiked Pickled Sweet Red Peppers.

Serves 4

Wine Selection

Oak aged Sauvignon Blanc to match the smoky bacon and tomato flavours woudl be a good choice. But a gamey Shiraz could also be a good style for contrast. Our wine suggestion: Longridge of Hawkes Bay Oak Aged Sauvignon Blanc or Robard & Butler Shiraz.

Sun-dried Tomato Paste

150 grams sun-dried
  tomatoes in oil
2 cloves garlic, peeled
few sprigs fresh parley,
  preferably Italian
1 small tomato (or
  medium), roasted

few shakes Tabasco sauce
1-2 tblsp grated fresh
  Parmesan cheese
freshly ground black
  pepper and salt

1 Drain the tomatoes well of their oil, but keep the oil. In a food processor or small blender put the tomatoes, garlic, parsley, tomato and Tabasco Sauce, and process until the mixture is smooth.

2 Add the reserved oil or fresh olive oil to reach a smooth paste. You may need an extra 1-2 tblsp depending on how well drained the tomatoes were. Add the Parmesan cheese to taste. If you like it stronger in flavour, then add all the Parmesan. Season if wished with pepper and a smidge of salt.

3 Keep refrigerated. It will last for about 2 weeks, unless you are like us and eat it all.

4 To roast the tomato, place it on a piece of foil on a tray and bake at 220°C for about 12-15 minutes until it is well browned and cooked.

Makes about 3/4 cup

Cook's Tip

If you cannot obtain sun-dried tomato paste in your supermarket, here is my recipe. I add a roasted fresh tomato because I find it gives a smooth sweet taste to the paste.

Basil Spiked Pickled Sweet Red Peppers

Juicy red peppers preserved in a sweet brine with fresh basil make a great partner for the Poussin. Use them also in tossed green salads or pasta dishes.

6 large shiny sweet red peppers
2 large onions, peeled
6 juicy cloves garlic, peeled
1/4 cup olive oil
1 tblsp French Mustard
2 tblsp capers
1 cup white wine vinegar
1/2 cup sugar
4-6 leaves fresh basil

1 Grill the red peppers under a fierce heat until they are blackened. Turn to ensure even cooking. *I cook mine on 240°C fan grill and they take next to no time.* Allow them to cool in a sealed plastic bag for about 10 minutes before peeling away their charred skin. Core and deseed the peppers. Cut each pepper into 8.

2 Cut the onions into thin wedge shapes and slice the garlic in half.

3 Heat the oil in a frying pan and add the onions, cooking over a moderate heat until they are soft but not brown.

4 Add the peppers, garlic, French mustard, capers, vinegar and sugar, and allow the mixture to simmer for about 10 minutes.

5 Bottle into hot dry jars. When cold, stir in the torn basil leaves and seal. Keep refrigerated.

Makes 3 350-gram jars

Olive Oil & Sauterne Cake

This cake was developed by a restaurant in California called Chez Panisse. It has a light yet dense texture with a smooth citrus and fruity flavour. Enjoy it with the Syllabub.

1 cup flour
1/2 tsp salt
1/2 tsp baking powder
5 eggs yolks
3/4 cup caster sugar
1/2 cup good quality fruity virgin olive oil
grated rind of 1 lemon and 1 orange
7 egg whites
1/2 tsp cream of tartar
1/2 cup sauterne or dessert wine

1 Sift the flour, salt and baking powder together and set aside.

2 In a clean bowl beat the egg yolks with half the caster sugar until the mixture is quite pale and creamy. Beat in the oil and citrus rinds to make a thick smooth mixture.

3 In another scrupulously clean bowl, beat the egg whites and cream of tartar with a clean beater until they form soft peaks. Gradually beat in the remaining caster sugar and continue to beat until the mixture is meringue-like.

4 Fold the egg yolks, flour and sauterne into the egg whites. Pour the mixture into a well greased, floured and lined 23 cm loose bottomed round cake tin.

5 Bake at 180°C for 20 minutes, then lower the heat to 160°C for a second 20 minutes. Place a buttered piece of paper, buttered side down, on the cake and turn the oven off. Allow the cake to cool down for a further 10 minutes. Remove and cool on a cake rack. The cake will sink a little in the centre, so don't panic. When cold, remove paper and turn out.

6 Serve cut in wedges accompanied with large spoonfuls of Citrus Syllabub.

Serves 8

Citrus Syllabub

Syllabubs are indeed very old-fashioned. They date back to around the 17th century when milk was whipped with egg whites and ale to make a frothy drink. Sounds awful if you ask me! This version is a little richer using cream, yoghurt and sweet wine with a touch of brandy. It can be made quite some time in advance, up to 8 hours.

1/2 cup dessert wine
1 tblsp dry sherry
2 tblsp brandy
1/4 cup caster sugar
grated rind each 1 lemon and orange
1 1/4 cups cream
1/2 cup non-fat yoghurt

1 Put the wine, sherry, brandy, sugar and citrus rinds into a bowl and allow them to stand for about 30 minutes.

2 Whip the chilled cream slowly with an electric beater until it becomes frothy. Gradually beat in the alcohol and continue to beat until the mixture becomes thick and forms soft peaks. Quickly beat in the yoghurt.

3 Spoon the mixture into a serving dish and place in the refrigerator to chill for about 2 hours.

Serve with the Sauterne Cake.

Serves 6

> **Wine Selection**
> *Try this with a Botrytised dessert wine. It should have intense fruit flavours and good acid. Use the same wine in the dish. Our wine suggestion: dessert wines from the Corbans Private Bin range.*

Lamb with Artichoke Hearts in a Tomato Broth

The idea for this lovely dish comes from Jacqui Dixon, who owns the food importing company Sabato with her husband Phil. Jacqui made something similar for us one night claiming that it was made from all the bits left over in the fridge. Some leftovers!

500 grams lamb fillets
100-gram packet kassler (smoked pork), prosciutto or bacon rashers
2 tblsp olive oil
1 cup finely sliced shallots
4 cloves garlic, crushed but not peeled
1 cup chicken stock

500 grams chopped juicy summer tomatoes
400-gram can artichoke hearts, well drained and halved
12 stuffed olives
1 bay leaf
500-gram packet frozen broad beans
fresh ground black pepper

1 Wrap the lamb fillets individually in the kassler slices and secure each one with a toothpick. Set aside. The kassler slices will not completely cover the lamb so do not worry. If using bacon, stretch the rashers with the back of a large cook's knife beforehand to ensure the rashers are not too thick.

2 Heat the olive oil in a deep heatproof casserole and cook the shallots and garlic for about 3 minutes.

Cook's Tips

- *Shallots have a lovely mild onion flavour. Use about ³⁄₄ cup chopped onions in their place.*
- *Fresh tomatoes are best, as tinned tomatoes will not give the same flavour to this dish. If you have the time, blanch and peel the tomatoes – I'm afraid I rarely do!*

3 Add the lamb fillets, turning in the oil to brown.

4 Add the chicken stock, tomatoes, artichoke hearts, olives and bay leaf. Simmer on top of the stove for about 35-40 minutes until the lamb is well cooked.

5 Transfer the cooking liquid to a clean saucepan and boil until reduced by half. Return to the casserole.

6 Blanch and peel the broad beans and add to the lamb. Reheat and season with pepper.

7 Serve over couscous. Directions for cooking are given on the packet, and use stock not water. Season well with salt and a knob of butter.

Serves 6

Wine Selection

Artichokes are quite a difficult wine match but a well oaked Chardonnay should go well with the slight sweetness of the tomatoes and nuttiness of broad beans. Our wine suggestion: Corbans Private Bin Gisborne Chardonnay or Longridge of Hawkes Bay Chardonnay.

Blueberry Frangipane Tart

One of my favourite desserts. Try lightly toasting the ground almonds for an even nuttier flavour.

2 sheets pre-rolled butter pastry (Ernest Adams is good)

Filling

75 grams butter

¼ cup caster sugar

2 eggs

few drops almond essence

¾ cup ground almonds

½ cup self rising flour

2 cups fresh blueberries

1 Roll the pastry sheets together and use them to line the base and sides of a 24-cm fluted flan dish. Bake blind at 200°C for about 12-15 minutes. Remove the baking blind material. *If the pastry is still a little moist, return to the oven for a further 2-3 minutes or until cooked.*

2 Filling. Beat the butter and sugar together until creamy. Add the eggs and almond essence and beat well. Fold in the almonds and sifted flour.

You can beat the butter, sugar and eggs together in a food processor until creamy and then pulse in the almonds and flour.

3 Spread half the mixture over the hot pastry. *The heat will help spread the filling, but work quickly.* Sprinkle over the blueberries. Dot with remaining filling. The filling will spread as it bakes so do not worry if you do not think there is enough.

4 Bake at 200°C for 10 minutes then lower the heat to 190°C for a further 20 minutes or until cooked. Serve warm with lashings of whipped cream or yoghurt.

Serves 6-8

Variations

Try using sliced apricots, peaches or blackberrries in place of the blueberries.

Wine Selection

Rich in flavour, but deliciously light to eat, match this with a sparkling Spumante. Our wine suggestion: Italiano Spumante.

Menu

Carrot & Cumin Soup with Orange

Saffron Pilaf with Crispy Lemon Grass Pork

Peaches in Merlot & Vanilla

ᎦᎦᎦᎦᎦ

Carrot & Cumin Soup with Orange

You need sweet carrots for this easy-to-make soup that can be made in advance and reheated before serving.

3 tblsp olive oil

2 medium onions, peeled and chopped

2 cloves garlic, peeled and crushed

2 tsp cumin seeds (or ground cumin)

7 medium carrots, peeled and grated

4 ½ cups chicken stock

1 ½ cups orange juice

salt

freshly ground black pepper

cream for garnish (whipped fresh, sour or creme fraiche)

fresh chives and cumin seeds to garnish

1 Heat the oil in a saucepan and cook the onion and garlic for about 3-5 minutes over a moderate heat until soft. Add the cumin seeds and cook a further 3-4 minutes.

2 Add the grated carrot and stock and bring slowly to the boil. Lower heat, cover and simmer for about 20 minutes until the carrot is tender.

3 Remove from the heat and purée in a food processor. Add the orange juice and season with salt and pepper.

4 Serve in warm bowls garnished with cream, chives and cumin seeds.

Serves 6

Wine Selection

Sweet with a touch of spice, this soup should go well with a medium Rielsing. Our wine suggestion: Stoneleigh Vineyard Marlborough Riesling.

Saffron Pilaf with Crispy Lemon Grass Pork

This magical pilaf is a wonderful combination of Jasmine rice gently scented with saffron from the Middle East, lemon grass from Thailand, ginger from Central Asia and completed with the basil and coriander.

*2 scotch fillet pork steaks
    or 3 pork schnitzels*

*1 stalk lemon grass,
    trimmed of green stalk*

3 tblsp olive oil

*2-cm piece fresh ginger,
    peeled and finely
    chopped*

*1 onion, peeled and finely
    chopped*

*2 big juicy cloves garlic,
    peeled and chopped*

2 cups Jasmine rice

¼ tsp saffron threads

¼ cup white wine

1¾ cups vegetable stock

*¼ cup each fresh basil and
    coriander leaves*

*100 grams shrimps or crab
    meat*

1 Trim any excess fat from the pork. Slice the steaks into very fine strips. Mince or finely chop the lemon grass. Mix 1 tablespoon of oil with the lemon grass and ginger and toss the pork in this mixture. Leave for 4 hours or overnight.

2 Heat the remaining olive oil in a heavy based frying pan and cook the onion for 5 minutes until softened but not brown. Add the garlic and cook for a further 2 minutes. Stir in the rice and coat in the oil.

3 Heat the saffron and wine together in the microwave for about 1 minute until the wine has become quite golden. Or put the wine and saffron in a saucepan and bring to boiling point. Remove from the heat and allow to stand for 2-3 minutes until golden in colour.

4 Add the wine and stock to the pan. Bring to the boil and then reduce the heat to a low temperature and allow the rice to barely simmer for 12-15 minutes until all the liquid has been absorbed.

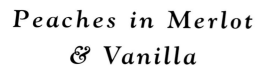

5 Cook the pork in a frying pan with a smidgen of oil until it is quite crispy. Be careful not to burn the ginger and lemon grass.

6 Toss through the torn basil and coriander leaves and chopped crab meat or shrimps. Arrange the meat on top of the pilaf and serve hot.

S e r v e s   6

Peaches in Merlot & Vanilla

A plummy light merlot is used to poach the peaches gently and to mellow with the subtle vanilla essences from the vanilla pod. It is a dessert that needs to be served well chilled. It is delicious when accompanied with a mixture of whipped cream and crushed amaretti biscuits (see page 67, Amaretti Cream).

1 cup water
1 cup caster sugar
2 cups merlot
1 vanilla pod
8 ripe peaches

1 In a saucepan put the water, sugar, merlot and vanilla pod and bring to the boil, stirring until the sugar dissolves. Allow to simmer for 5 minutes.

2 Peel, halve and stone the peaches. Cut into thick slices. Add to the hot wine and allow to poach over a moderate heat without boiling for about 10 minutes until the peaches are just about tender.

3 Remove from the heat and allow the peaches to stand for a further 10 minutes.

4 Transfer the peaches to a serving bowl or container and return the wine mixture to the saucepan. Boil until reduced by about ⅓.

5 Pour over the peaches and chill. Serve cold with the Amaretti Cream.

S e r v e s   6 - 8

Menu

Venison with Porcini Pesto

Baked Apricot & Apple Tart

⌐⌐⌐⌐⌐

Venison with Porcini Pesto

Porcini are wonderful earthy treasures also called ceps. They have a deep meaty, woodsy taste that will bring intense mushroom flavour to your cooking. As they are expensive I use them in a pesto style dish that will extend their use with many options for cooking. Venison steaks marinated in the soaking liquid of the delicate porcini mushrooms and served medium rare with the porcini pesto make a great meal.

20 grams dried porcini
*   mushrooms*
½ cup warm water
1 medium-sized tomato
1 small clove garlic, peeled
2 tblsp roasted pinenuts
¼ cup grated Italian
*   Parmesan cheese*

3-4 tblsp good virgin
*   olive oil*
2 large leaves fresh basil
4 venison steaks (cut and
*   thickness to your liking)*

1 Put the porcini mushrooms and water into a bowl and leave them to soak for about 30 minutes. Drain, reserving the liquid.

2 While the mushrooms are soaking, cut the tomato in half. Heat a drop or two of olive oil in a frying pan and cook the tomato on both sides until it is well browned and cooked.

3 In a small food processor or blender put the porcini mushrooms, tomato, garlic clove, pinenuts, Parmesan, olive oil and basil. Process until the mixture is well blended. Season with pepper and a smidge of salt if wished. Add more olive oil to reach the desired consistency if you prefer it thinner.

4 Keep the pesto in an airtight container in the refrigerator. Allow it to come to room temperature before using.

5 Arrange the venison steaks in a single layer in a dish and pour over the mushroom soaking liquid. Add a dash of Pinot Noir if wished and season it all well with pepper. Allow the steaks to marinate for about 2 hours in the refrigerator.

6 Cook the steaks over a high heat for about 3 minutes on each side. The steaks should be rare to medium rare (well done venison is tough and dry). Set aside and keep warm, standing for at least 1 minute before serving.

7 Add the marinating liquid to the pan and reduce by half. Pour over the steaks and serve with a dollop of the porcini pesto and a fresh basil leaf on top, drizzled with a smidge of balsamic vinegar if you have it.

Serves 4

Cook's Tip

If there is more pesto left, use it to top a crostini, tossed through pasta, or even spread on bread in place of butter with a slice of rare roast beef. Mix it into a quiche or frittata filling, or add a tablespoon or 2 to a gravy or sauce.

Wine Selection

The perfect partner for both venison and porcini is Pinot Noir. Its gamey mushroom flavour makes this a truly delicious combination. Our wine suggestion: The hard-to-find Corbans Cottage Block Pinot Noir. A great value alternative is the Robard & Butler Shiraz.

Baked Apricot & Apple Tart

Fresh summer apricots with crisp apples baked in a simple open tart make a scrummy dessert that takes little effort.

175 grams chilled butter, diced
2 cups flour
2 tblsp sugar
2-3 tblsp cold water

Filling

2 crunchy apples, peeled and finely sliced
300 grams apricots, halved, stoned and sliced
2 tblsp cornflour
2 tblsp runny honey
milk to glaze
2 tblsp sugar
extra honey to glaze (optional)

1 Pastry. Put the butter, flour and sugar into a food processor and process until the mixture resembles coarse crumbs. Add 2 tblsp of the water and pulse until the mixture forms small moist balls of dough. Add more water if necessary. *Do not process until the dough forms a single ball as this will over work the dough and make it quite tough.*

2 Turn out onto a floured board and bring together. Refrigerate for about 10 minutes while preparing the fruit. *This allows the pastry to relax, which means it will not shrink when you roll it out or be tough when you bake it.*

3 Roll the dough out to form a large circle, about 30 cm in diameter. Place the dough over a 24 cm fluted flan tin, leaving the excess hanging over the edge.

4 Toss the prepared fruit, cornflour and honey together and pile into the centre of the tart. Carefully bring the extra pastry up and over the edges of the tart. Brush the pastry with milk and then sprinkle the sugar over.

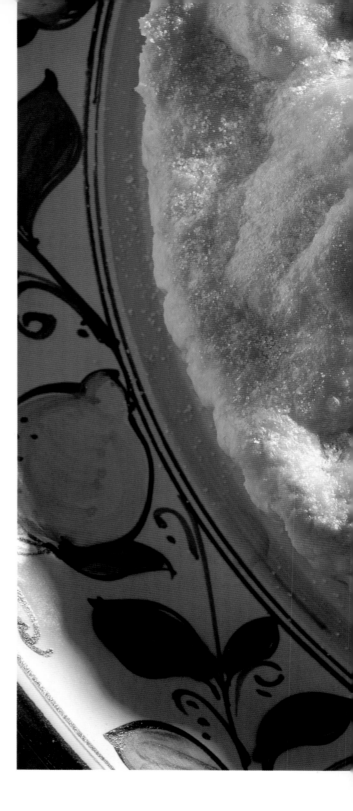

5 Bake at 190°C on fan bake or 210°C without a fan for 30 minutes.

6 Brush with extra honey when the tart comes out of the oven to glaze. Serve with lashings of cream or great dollops of yoghurt.

S e r v e s   6

Variations

- Use finely sliced fresh figs and apples.

- Use only apples and spice with cardamom, ginger or cinnamon.

- Add 1 tblsp of a matching liqueur to the honey when glazing just before serving.

Wine Selection

A late harvest wine that is not too rich or weighty is the best choice for this lovely fruit tart. Our wine suggestion: Corbans Private Bin Late Harvest Semillon Sauvignon Blanc.

Beef Fillet wrapped in Indian Flavours

Spicy Chickpea Patties with Apple & Mango Salsa

Fresh Date Tart Tatin

⟨⟨⟨⟨⟨

Beef Fillet wrapped in Indian Flavours

Wrap a tender beef fillet up in spicy Indian flavours and serve medium rare with a fresh Apple and Mango Salsa and accompaniments like Chick Pea Patties, poppadoms and chutneys, and it becomes very special.

4 tblsp Indian flavour base
2 tblsp plain yoghurt
1 tsp freshly ground pepper
1-kg piece eye fillet

2 tblsp olive oil
¾ cup white wine
½ cup beef stock

1 Mix the Indian base with the yoghurt and pepper and spread over the eye fillet. Place in a plastic container, cover and leave to marinate overnight or for at least 4 hours.

Cook's Tip

Indian base mixes are available in jars and packets by several manufacturers, making the mixing of the spice blend much easier. On this occasion, Masterfoods 'Cuisine Essential, Indian' was used.

Wine Selection

Lots of intense spice in this dish will need a robust wine to match. Our wine suggestion: If you enjoy reds, try a Robard & Butler Shiraz; or a good white wine style would be the Longridge of Hawkes Bay Gewurztraminer.

2 Heat the olive oil in a roasting dish and add the beef. Turn over a high heat to brown on all sides. Transfer to a 170°C oven and cook for 25 minutes. Remove from the heat and set aside, covered, to stand for 10 minutes before carving.

3 Add the wine and beef stock to the pan and simmer over a moderate heat, stirring to lift any sediment from the pan. (You can thicken the sauce with 1 tsp cornflour mixed to a paste with water and simmer 1 minute longer if you wish.)

4 Carve the meat into thin slices and serve with the sauce, Chick Pea Patties and Apple and Mango Salsa. If desired, add poppadums and other chutneys.

Serves 6

Spicy Chickpea Patties

These spicy patties are a great change from the usual rice or potatoes. They were created for a wonderful meal at The Sheraton, Auckland, for the Food Writers annual dinner. I have tried to recreate them here.

1¼ cups chick peas
3 cloves garlic, peeled and crushed
2 tsp finely grated ginger
2 tsp garam masala
1 tsp salt

1 tsp turmeric and curry powder
2 eggs
clarified butter for pan-frying

1 Cover chickpeas with cold water and set aside to soak for about 4 hours.

2 Drain well. Bring a large pot of water to the boil and add the chickpeas. Simmer gently for 1 hour or until the chickpeas are well cooked. Drain, discarding any of the loose skins as well.

3 Put the chickpeas, garlic, ginger, garam masala, turmeric, curry powder and salt into a food processor and pulse until well chopped. Add the egg and process until well combined.

4 Mould the chick peas into patties. Heat the clarified butter and cook the patties on both sides until golden and crispy. Keep warm while preparing the remaining patties.

M a k e s   1 2 - 1 4

W i n e   S e l e c t i o n
Balance out the warm spicy tastes of the patties with a fresh fruity Riesling. Our wine suggestion: The latest release of the Stoneleigh Vineyard Marlborough Riesling.

Apple & Mango Salsa

Fresh apples diced with lemon juice, mint and cider vinegar make a refreshing accompaniment to this meal.

2 apples, peeled and very finely diced

2 mangoes, peeled and diced

1 tblsp cider vinegar

2 tblsp mint, chopped

1 spring onion, well trimmed and finely chopped

grated rind 1 lemon

Mix the diced apples and mangoes together with the cider vinegar, mint, spring onion, and lemon rind.

M a k e s   a b o u t   1 1/2   c u p s

Fresh Date Tart Tatin

Fresh dates are so sticky (yum) that they are
great to have on their own, but when cooked
with cardamom and bananas in an upside-down
tart they are particularly moreish.

1½ cups flour
½ tsp baking powder
1-2 tsp ground cardamom
100 grams butter
3-4 tblsp chilled water
2 bananas
12-14 fresh dates, halved lengthways and stoned
25 grams butter
2 tblsp brown sugar

1 Put the flour, baking powder, cardamom and
butter into a food processor and process until
the mixture resembles fine crumbs.

2 With the machine running, add about 3 tblsp
water and then pulse until the mix forms small
moist balls of dough. Add more water if necessary.
Turn out and bring together. Refrigerate for
15 minutes.

3 Peel and slice the bananas into 1-cm thick
slices.

4 Heat the butter in a 20-23 cm ovenproof
frying pan and stir in the brown sugar. When
the mixture is bubbling, arrange the dates and
bananas in the base of the pan. Leave the dates
and bananas over a low heat while rolling out
the pastry.

5 Roll out the pastry to about 1 cm larger
than the frying pan and roll over the dates
and bananas, tucking in the sides of the pastry.

6 Transfer to a 200°C oven and bake for
15 minutes or until the pastry is golden
and cooked.

7 Stand for 5 minutes before turning upside-down
on a serving plate. Serve warm with cream
scented with rosewater or lemon rind, whichever
you prefer.

S e r v e s 6

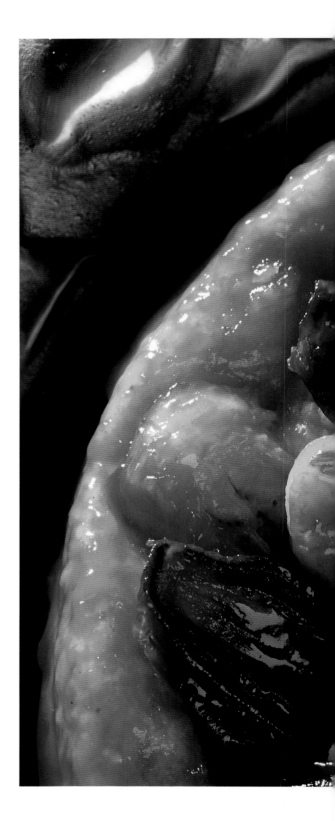

Impromptu Dining

Friends have dropped in to say hello and you've asked them to stay for dinner. Don't panic! So long as it is all fun, it doesn't really matter what you prepare and enjoy. These ideas are made with a few items from the store cupboard, and maybe a couple of fresh ingredients.

The Soufflé

Eggs can make an instant meal and with a little bit of cheese you can turn them into something wonderful, like a soufflé. A soufflé takes hardly any time to prepare (it can be made and eaten within an hour) and is simple and elegant.

*butter to grease the dish
with*
*2 tblsp semolina, grated
Parmesan cheese or
breadcrumbs*
50 grams butter
3 tblsp flour
1¼ cups milk

4 eggs, separated
1 tblsp Dijon mustard
*1 cup grated or diced
cheese*
*3-4 rashers bacon, diced
and lightly cooked
(optional)*

1 Lightly grease a 1.5-litre soufflé or casserole-style dish with butter or oil and dust with semolina, Parmesan cheese or breadcrumbs.

2 Melt the butter in a saucepan and add the flour. Cook over a moderate heat for about 2 minutes until frothy.

3 Stir in the milk and cook, stirring until the sauce has thickened. Allow it to bubble away for about 1 minute. Remove from the heat and allow to cool slightly.

4 Beat in the egg yolks, Dijon mustard, cheese and bacon (if using).

5 In a clean bowl beat the egg whites until they form stiff peaks. *Add ¼ tsp cream of tartar if you have it as this will help increase the volume.*

6 Take a large spoonful of the beaten egg whites and stir it gently into the sauce mixture. *This is to bring the two mixtures to a similar consistency, making it easier to fold them together without losing too much of the air that has been beaten into the egg whites.*

7 Gently fold the sauce mixture into the remaining egg whites.

8 Pour the mixture over the back of a spoon, to avoid bursting too many of those precious air bubbles, into the prepared dish.

9 Place the soufflé on a pre-heated tray in a 200°C oven and instantly turn down to 180°C. Cook for 35 minutes or until cooked. A slight shake will tell you if it is cooked: a violent wobble means that it needs more time; a slight wibble (a small wobble) in the centre means that it is ready. A soufflé should have a little of the mixture just undercooked in the centre to act as a sauce for the remainder.

10 Serve immediately with sliced fresh tomato or salad greens tossed in vinaigrette.

Serves 4

Variations

- Add a few sliced sun-dried red peppers or tomatoes.

- Add herbs (onion flavours like chives go well with eggs).

- Add sliced, cooked mushrooms or sliced reconstituted porcini mushrooms.

- Try capers finely chopped with really tasty cheese.

- Smoked salmon, diced and folded through before cooking.

- Chopped canned asparagus, great with cheese too.

- Vary the cheese: try crumbled feta or blue vein, diced or grated Edam or Gouda, or diced soft cheese such as a Brie or Camembert.

Cook's Tip
Mustards vary from warm and sweet to very hot, so pick the one that most suits you. Yellow mustard seeds are used to make the mild American-style mustards, while yellow and brown seeds are blended for English mustards. The brown seeds are used in Dijon mustard, which is a tangy sweet mustard that goes well with cheese. It's good to have a variety on hand in your cupboards.

Wine Selection
Choose a wine to match to more dominant flavours of your soufflé. A red wine will go well with mushrooms, cheese and sun-dried red peppers; a Sauvignon Blanc will match salmon, asparagus, herbs and onions. Our wine suggestion: Longridge of Hawkes Bay Cabernet/Merlot or Stoneleigh Vineyard Marlborough Sauvignon Blanc.

½ cup basic vinaigrette (see page 78)

Dressing

½ cup basic vinaigrette (see page 78)
2-3 cloves garlic, peeled and crushed

1 Line a baking tray with foil. Brush the aubergine on both sides with olive oil and place in a single layer on the tray. Arrange the courgettes, beans and red peppers on the tray and brush these with olive oil.

2 Grill them under your oven's highest heat (I use 240° fan grill) until the vegetables have begun to blacken slightly. Remove the peppers as they colour up and turn the aubergines to grill the other side.

3 When all the vegetables are grilled, cut them into smaller pieces and place in a large dish. Core and dice the tomatoes and add. Flake the tuna and toss in with the capers and olives.

4 Brush the French stick slices with olive oil and grill on both sides until they are lightly toasted. Cut in half and toss through the salad with the dressing until just blended.

5 Serve garnished with roughly chopped or torn fresh herbs such as parsley, basil or chives and with a basket of warm crusty breads.

S e r v e s   4

Dressing

Put the vinaigrette and garlic in a small processor or shaker blend well.

Wine Selection

Grilled vegetables and tuna are a great match for oak-aged Sauvignon Blanc. Choose one that has good herbaceous fruit flavours. Our wine suggestion: Longridge of Hawkes Bay Sauvignon Blanc.

Roasted Summer Vegetable & Tuna Toss

Use your own selection of salad vegetables for this and grill them until lightly blistered. Toss them with a can of tuna and a rich garlic-flavoured vinaigrette, and serve warm in large bowls. Great for quick eating or using up vegetable leftovers from the fridge.

1 medium-sized aubergine, thinly sliced
olive oil for brushing
3-4 courgettes
handful of green beans
1 each red and green pepper, quartered and de-seeded
4 large juicy summer tomatoes

185-gram can tuna, drained
2 tblsp capers
olives, optional for 4
½ French stick, thinly sliced
herbs for garnish (parsley, basil or chives)

Omelette Salad

By combining these great favourites you can quickly prepare a reasonably jazzy salad good enough to enjoy with unexpected guests.

salad greens for 4
about 12 olives, black or green
summer salad vegetables such as tomatoes or sprouts
4 eggs

few chopped spring onions or chives
4 sun-dried tomatoes in oil, finely diced
1 tblsp oil or butter
vinaigrette (see page 78)

1 Wash the salad greens and dry in a lettuce spinner or in a tea towel. Freshen them for 5 minutes in the refrigerator if you have time. Arrange the torn salad greens on a large platter and toss in the olives, summer vegetables and spring onions or chives.

2 Beat the eggs together well with a good pinch of salt in a large bowl. Add the sun-dried tomatoes and beat well.

3 Heat the oil in a non-stick frying pan or an omelette pan. When hot, pour in the omelette mixture and stir vigorously with a fork for about 15 seconds. Leave the omelette to cook until the top has become dull. If you can, flip the omelette to give the other side about half a minute.

4 Turn the omelette onto a wooden board and slice very finely. Toss through the salad. Serve the salad with vinaigrette on the side. It would be nice to make the vinaigrette with lemon infused olive oil, if you have it.

5 Serve with pita bread that has been brushed liberally with butter, placed under a hot grill and cooked until lightly golden and hot. Season well with ground black pepper. Or you could serve with new potatoes tossed in herb butter.

S e r v e s   4

W i n e   S e l e c t i o n

Match the taste of summer in this dish with a refreshing Sauvignon Blanc for a delicious combination of crisp flavours. Our wine suggestion: Stoneleigh Vineyard Marlborough Sauvignon Blanc.

Chicken Italian-style

Pan-fried chicken breasts topped with the flavours of Italy – delicious!

1 tblsp capers
¼ cup black or green olives, pitted
2 sun-dried red peppers or tomatoes, finely sliced
4 single breasts of chicken

2 tblsp each chopped parsley and marjoram
2 tblsp olive oil or butter
2 cloves garlic, peeled and crushed

1 Chop the capers, olives and sun-dried red peppers or tomatoes, and mix with the parsley and marjoram.

2 Using a mallet, flatten the chicken a little. Heat the oil in a frying pan and cook the chicken over a low heat for about 25-30 minutes, turning occasionally until cooked. Add the garlic 3-4 minutes before the chicken finishes cooking. Season well with pepper.

3 Arrange each chicken piece on a plate and top with a quarter of the caper mixture. Drizzle with a little of the oil from the sun-dried foods if wished.

Serves 4

Wine Selection

This simple but delicious combination of chicken and vegetables should be matched with a Sauvignon Blanc with or without oak, whichever you prefer. Our wine suggestion: Try a bottle each of Stoneleigh Vineyard Marlborough Sauvignon Blanc and the Longridge of Hawkes Bay Sauvignon Blanc to test for yourself!

Bacon Gnocchi

Adding a little bacon to semolina gnocchi makes it a fabulous tasty meal, ideal to serve in summer with a crisp salad or hearty winter vegetables mid-year.

3-4 rashers bacon, trimmed
   of rind and diced
1 onion, finely diced or
   minced
1 tblsp olive oil
3 cups milk
¾ cup semolina
1 tsp salt

1 cup grated cheddar
   cheese
50-100 grams diced goat's
   cheese (optional)
1 egg, beaten well
1 slice of bread, crumbed
¼ cup cream (lite cream if
   you prefer)

1 Cook the bacon and onion in the olive oil for about 4-5 minutes. Set aside.

2 Heat the milk in a large jug in the microwave on 100% power for 5 minutes or until boiling. Stir in the semolina and return to the microwave for a further 3 minutes on 100% power and stir occasionally. Continue to cook only if the mixture is not very thick.

3 Stir in the grated cheese, salt, goat's cheese and half the bacon mixture.

4 Pour the mixture out into a well greased 20 cm x 20 cm slice tin. Allow to stand in the fridge for 2 hours.

5 Use a cookie cutter to cut the gnocchi into rounds of about 3 cm or similar. Use the off-cuts to press into the base of a shallow baking dish, such as a quiche dish. Arrange the round pieces on top. Brush liberally with the beaten egg and sprinkle over the breadcrumbs and remaining bacon mixture.

6 Pour over the cream. Bake at 180°C for 35-40 minutes until piping hot and golden.

7 Serve immediately with a salad.

Serves 4

Cook's Tip

If you do not have a microwave, use a saucepan to make the semolina. You will have to stir the mixture most of the time, to prevent it catching. Microwaves are excellent for cooking with milk.

Wine Selection

Rich and cheesy, with smoky bacon flavours, this dish would be great with either an oak-aged Sauvignon Blanc or a lightly oaked Chardonnay. Our wine suggestion: Longridge of Hawkes Bay Oak Aged Sauvignon Blanc or the Corbans Estate Gisborne Chardonnay.

Pasta Plus

Pasta is more than the food of the nineties; it is healthy, convenient and good value, and appealing to both our taste buds and our pockets. There are many books about what to cook with pasta, but the reality is almost anything can be put with pasta to make it into a fabulous meal.

Mussels & Olives

Heat a 425-gram tin of Italian-style tomatoes and blend through 500 grams marinated cooked green mussels, and ½ cup stuffed olives. Season well with basil and lemon juice. Toss through and serve with freshly cooked pasta for 4.

Courgette & Buttered Pinenuts

Trim, wash and grate 4 medium-sized courgettes. Heat about 25 grams butter in a frying pan and toss in 4 rashers of diced bacon. When almost cooked, add a couple of handfuls of pinenuts and cook, tossing, until toasted. Add the courgettes and simmer for 1 minute. Stir in ½ cup sour cream and season with salt and pepper. Toss through freshly cooked pasta for 4. Serve with Parmesan cheese.

Sun-dried Tomatoes on Pasta

Cook the pasta until al dente. Drain well and toss through several tablespoons of sun-dried tomato paste. Season with pepper and add whole black olives and plenty of freshly torn green basil. Serve with Parmesan cheese. Pan fried bacon or slices of rare beef or lamb are also good with this. Roasted garlic (page 24) is also great to toss through with the sun-dried tomato paste.

Snowpeas & Chicken & Blue Cheese

Blanch 200 grams snowpeas and/or asparagus, and pan fry 4 rashers of bacon, then chop roughly. Thinly slice 2 cooked chicken breasts and in a frying pan put snowpeas or asparagus, bacon, chicken, 2 tblsp wholeseed mustard, 1 cup cream and ½ cup chicken stock. Warm through and add 100 grams sliced blue cheese. Toss through freshly cooked hot pasta and top each serving with a gently cooked poached egg, if wished. Garnish with chives.

Walnut Paste & Bacon

This is an all-time favourite in our house. Walnut paste is readily available from supermarkets or good delicatessens. Pan-fry 3-4 rashers of finely diced bacon with a clove or 2 of garlic in some olive oil. Add 3 finely chopped spring onions, ¼ cup Madeira, 1 cup chicken stock and 2 tblsp walnut paste. Once hot stir in about ¼ cup crème fraîche or sour cream, and simmer for 1 minute. Pour over freshly cooked hot pasta for 4. Serve with Parmesan cheese and parsley.

Wine Selection

A wide selection of wines will work with these pasta dishes. The Mussels & Olives and Sun-dried Tomatoes dishes would be good with a Sauvignon Blanc, and try the Courgette & Pinenuts and Snowpeas & Blue Cheese with a light Chardonnay. Our wine suggestions: Stoneleigh Vineyard Marlborough Sauvignon Blanc, Robard & Butler Shiraz and Corbans Estate Gisborne Chardonnay.

Dine & Dash Desserts

Try these ideas for desserts in a hurry:

- Toss raspberries, blueberries and strawberries together with a little sweet white wine or framboise and serve with dollops of yoghurt or cream. Garnish with violets.

- Make a melon salad special with thin slices of canteloupe, rock and watermelon tossed with a little freshly squeezed lemon and orange juice.

- Toss sliced bananas in butter and pan-fry with a sprinkling of brown sugar and Kahlua. Serve with cream and passionfruit pulp.

- Whip a bottle of cream and blend with 1 cup yoghurt and fold through fresh raspberries.

- Process half a dozen amaretti biscuits with a tablespoon brown sugar and a 70 gram packet chopped walnuts or shelled pistachios. Blend in an egg yolk. Pile the mixture into halved and stoned peaches or nectarines and bake in $\frac{1}{2}$ cup white wine in the oven for 45 minutes. Serve with whipped cream.

Icecream toppings are always a favourite. Have good ice cream and some fruit and top with one of these:

- Melt 125 grams chopped cooking chocolate with $\frac{1}{4}$ cup each of cocoa powder, water and cream. When melted, pour over good vanilla icecream and serve.

- Melt 25 grams butter in a saucepan and add a 70-gram packet chopped walnuts and 2 tblsp each of brown sugar, honey and whisky. Add a dash of cream if wished.

- Melt 25 grams butter in a saucepan. Add a well chopped 70-gram packet hazelnuts and toss in the butter to brown. Stir in $\frac{1}{2}$ cup apricot jam, a good dash of sherry and cream and simmer a minute.

- Blend 2 cups of your favourite berries with a spoonful of icing sugar until smooth.

Fruit & Cheese Combinations

If you have a little of both, these are some of the nicest combinations to serve after an impromptu dinner:

- raspberries and blueberries with camembert.

- pears and apples with blue cheeses.

- peaches and apricots with mascarpone and amaretti biscuits.

- pears with Parmesan.

- blackberries with strong tasty-style cheddar.

- plums and cherries with strong blues.

- pawpaw, peaches and apricots with brie and triple cream cheeses.

The 'Fast Food' Store Cupboard

Keeping a well-stocked pantry is essential today. It saves on time; is a constant source of inspiration; and provides a safety net for emergency entertaining.

Many items, such as pestos and sun-dried tomato pastes, olives and biscotti, which were once only deli lines, are now readily available in supermarkets. They are premium ingredients that can be made at home, but are certainly time-savers for the busy cook if already in your pantry. The following is a basic list of what I keep handy.

Dry Cupboard

Oils Good olive oils for dressings and pan-frying. Sesame, too, for jazzing up Asian flavours.

Vinegar White and red wine, cider, balsamic and sherry.

Mustard Wholeseed, a sweeter-style Dijon and a hot English one.

Spices Buy small quantities and use up. Keep cardamom or ginger (great with fruits), cumin, coriander, turmeric, garam masala, cayenne or chilli and a good curry powder. Don't forget sea salt, such as Maldon, and plenty of peppercorns.

Herbs Use them fresh, except for dill – it's partly OK!

Rices You need basmati for Indian flavours, jasmine for Asian dishes and desserts, and arborio for Italian foods. Plus boxes of couscous and bulgar wheat for alternatives. A box of polenta is also a great standby.

Alcohol Always use good wines, you will find that cheap wines become bitter. Plus sherry and brandy.

Sauces Worcestershire, soy, hoisin, Tabasco and a good homemade tomato sauce.

Condiments Sun-dried tomatoes and red peppers (in oil or pastes), walnut paste, olives (black and green), capers, gherkins, sambal oelek (chilli paste), curry pastes (Thai flavours). And good jams, like raspberry and apricot.

Pasta Lots of pasta in varying shapes.

Cans A whole stash of tomatoes and variants, tomato paste, coconut milk or cream, plus a sundry mix of cannellini beans, kidney beans, artichoke hearts, tuna, salmon and anchovies.

Fruits Something like apricots in brandy is always a good dessert standby.

Odds Crackers, pretzels, crostini, garlic, potatoes, onions, sugars and all the baking basics.

The fridge

Creams, either sour, fresh or fraîche, yoghurt, milk, butter (plain and unsalted), cheeses – a good mix of cheddar, white rinded and a blue.

The freezer

Ice for drinks, bacon, all your nuts (almonds, pinenuts, etc.), homemade stocks, good vanilla ice-cream and some frozen vegetables, such as beans. Packets of pre-rolled pastries, including puff and short crust.

Romantic Menus

Many of us are romantic at heart. Let's face it, there's nothing nicer in the world than falling in love and the wonderful things that happen. Don't stop being romantic. Make dates in your year, like anniversaries, Valentine's Day and birthdays, special and plan a little romance with flowers, cards and a dinner.

Poached Scallops in a Lime-Scented Broth

A simple meal to prepare and very elegant for a romantic dinner.

2 cups seafood or vegetable stock	50 grams shiitake mushrooms, finely sliced
1 kaffir lime leaf	½ bunch spinach, washed and trimmed
1 stalk lemon grass, trimmed	
2 spring onions, trimmed	250 grams fresh scallops or firm white fish fillets
½ head bok choy	

1 Put the stock and kaffir lime leaf into a large pot and bring to a simmer for 5 minutes.

2 Add lemon grass and spring onions to stock and simmer a further 5 minutes.

3 Add the mushrooms. Tear the spinach and bok choy leaves into pieces and add to the pan. Simmer until the leaves have wilted and the mixture is hot.

4 Clean and wash the scallops and add to the saucepan. Poach the scallops for 3-4 minutes in the hot broth. *Do not overcook as they will become rubbery.* If using fish fillets, cut the fillets into pieces the size of scallops and poach the same way.

5 Serve in large bowls over a mound of boiled Jasmine rice, garnished with coriander leaves.

Serves 2

Cook's Tip

- *Shiitake mushrooms make this a special meal. Use ordinary mushrooms if you do not have these available. You could also substitute dried shiitake mushrooms if you wish. Use about 8-10, soaking them in warm water for 10-15 minutes before slicing.*
- *Kaffir lime leaves can be purchased dried from supermarkets or Asian food shops.*

Wine Selection

Scallops and Riesling are a great combination, and the lime broth will emphasise the limey fruit flavours of the wine. Try a dry style with delicate lime-lemon fruit. Our wine suggestion: The latest release of Stoneleigh Vineyard Marlborough Riesling.

A Real Romantic Would

- ❤ Send flowers and not yellow roses, they mean forsaken love!
- ❤ Send a love note on the hour for the whole work day on St Valentine's Day.
- ❤ Play romantic music while enjoying dinner.
- ❤ Sprinkle rose petals over the table cloth and have roses as a gift at the end of a meal.
- ❤ Go on picnics in summer with bubbles and yummy food that's easy to prepare. Chicken, fresh bread, cheeses and fresh fruits.
- ❤ Have cosy winter nights in front of blazing warm fires.
- ❤ Send a card with loving messages at times other than St Valentine's Day.
- ❤ Scent cards with favourite perfumes.
- ❤ Go away on Mystery weekends to relaxing hideaway retreats.
- ❤ Leave cute love notes in hidden places to show you care.
- ❤ Serve breakfast (and maybe lunch!) in bed.

Lamb Noisettes with Madeira Cream Sauce

This recipe makes lamb special – it is my all-time favourite.

25 grams unsalted butter

4 lamb noisettes

½ onion (or 6 shallots), peeled and finely chopped

¼ cup Madeira or medium sherry

½ cup cream

1 tsp cornflour

½ cup chicken or vegetable stock

2 tblsp chopped chives or tarragon

pepper to season

1 Heat the butter in a frying pan and add the noisettes. Cook over a moderate heat for 4-5 minutes on each side until lightly browned. Do not overcook – they should be served pink.

2 Once cooked, remove from the pan. Add the onion or shallots and cook for about 3-4 minutes over a lower heat until softened.

3 Add the Madeira or sherry and bring to the boil. Simmer 3 minutes.

4 Add the cream and continue to boil until the mixture has reduced by half.

5 Mix the cornflour and stock together. Stir into the sauce and cook until thickened. Add the chives and tarragon and season with pepper.

6 Return the noisettes to the pan to warm them through. Serve with fresh vegetables.

Serves 2

Cook's Tip

Your butcher will usually prepare noisettes for you. If you have to make your own, buy loin chops and remove the bone. Wrap the tail around the eye fillet and secure with a toothpick. This is not quite the real thing but fairly close.

Wine Selection

You could match this dish with a ripe fruity Cabernet/ Merlot or try serving it with a big, bold, oaky Chardonnay. Our wine suggestions: Longridge of Hawkes Bay Cabernet/Merlot and Cooks Winemakers Reserve Chardonnay.

Oyster & Pepper Pie

Delicious and very special. Try Nelson Bay oysters – just divine!

2 sheets pre-rolled short pastry

25 grams butter

1 clove garlic, peeled and crushed

2 rashers bacon, trimmed of rind and diced

½ x 400-gram tin artichoke hearts

2 tblsp chopped parsley

¼ cup chopped spring onions

1 tsp chopped green peppercorns

dash brandy and cream

3 egg yolks

2 dozen oysters, shucked and drained

freshly ground black pepper

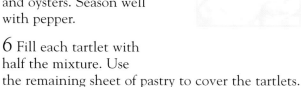

1 Use 1 sheet of pastry to line the bases of 2 x 10 cm flan tins. Place in the fridge while preparing the filling.

2 Melt the butter in a frying pan. Add the garlic and bacon and cook for 3-5 minutes over a moderate heat until the bacon is cooked.

3 Add the artichokes, spring onions and peppercorns and toss until liquid has evaporated.

4 Add the brandy (and if game, flambé). Once the flames have gone or after about 2 minutes, add a good dash of cream and reduce by about half.

5 Remove from the heat and allow to cool for 5 minutes. Fold through the egg yolks, parsley and oysters. Season well with pepper.

6 Fill each tartlet with half the mixture. Use the remaining sheet of pastry to cover the tartlets. Seal securely and brush with milk to glaze.

7 Have an oven tray hot in the oven. Bake the pies at 220°C for 10 minutes and then reduce to 180°C for a further 10-15 minutes until the pies are golden and hot.

Serve hot or cold. Serves 2

Wine Selection

Chardonnay and oysters – what could be better? Pick a big, ripe, flavoursome wine with lots of toasty oak. Our wine suggestion: Try the bold Cooks Winemakers Reserve Chardonnay.

Pickled Ginger & Dried Shiitake Mushrooms over Salmon

This main course dish can be prepared in advance and then cooked when required, making it ideal for entertaining. Dried shiitake mushrooms are one of the most versatile dried mushrooms and are ideal to keep on hand in the kitchen.

4 dried shiitake mushrooms
¼ cup dry sherry or water
1 tblsp olive oil
2 salmon steaks
   (150-200 grams each)
1 small clove garlic, peeled
   and mashed
6 sheets filo pastry
50 grams melted butter

1 spring onions, trimmed
   and finely sliced
1 tblsp pickled ginger,
   chopped
½ tsp sesame oil
2 tsp extra butter
sesame seeds to dust with
   (about 1 tblsp)

1 Put the shiitake mushrooms and hot sherry or water together in a bowl and set aside for 20-30 minutes until the mushrooms have reconstituted. Drain liquid and reserve. Slice the mushrooms finely.

2 Heat the oil in a frying pan and cook the salmon steaks for about 2 minutes only on each side and set aside on a board. Add the garlic to the pan and cook for 1-2 minutes. Set aside.

3 Carefully remove the skin from the salmon and then cut away the bone so that you have 2 pieces to each salmon steak.

4 Spread 1 sheet of filo pastry with a little melted butter and top with a second. Repeat with a third sheet of filo.

5 Place 1 salmon steak (2 pieces) onto the middle and at one end of the buttered filo sheets. Top with half the shiitake mushrooms, spring onion, pickled ginger and garlic. Drizzle over half the sesame oil and season well with pepper. Spoon on 1 tablespoon reserved sherry and 1 teaspoon extra butter.

6 Bring the shorter edges of filo over the salmon and then roll the salmon down the length of the filo sheets so that you have a secure parcel. Place onto a greased baking tray and brush the top of each parcel with melted butter and sprinkle over a few sesame seeds. Repeat with remaining ingredients.

7 Bake at 220°C for 10 minutes or until the filo is golden and the salmon just cooked.

8 Serve warm with a baby leaf green salad.

Serves 2

Wine Selection

The salmon in this dish takes on the sweet and spicy flavour of the pickled ginger. Match it with a medium Riesling, or if you prefer a dry style, a rich, buttery Chardonnay. Our wine suggestions: Corbans Private Bin Chardonnay, or the great value Corbans Estate Marlborough Riesling.

Strawberry Toffee Tarts

Buttery pastry filled with chocolate, mascarpone and strawberries glazed with toffee; sounds sensational and tastes that way too!

*1 sheet pre-rolled Ernest
    Adams Butter Pastry*
*50 grams dark cooking
    chocolate, melted*
½ cup chilled cream
½ punnet strawberries
1 cup sugar

*150 grams mascarpone
    cheese*
*grated rind of 1 lemon or
    orange*
icing sugar to taste
2 tblsp water

1 Use the pastry to line the base and sides of 2 or 3 x 10-cm tartlet tins. You will be able to cover two out of the sheet; and if you carefully re-roll the off-cuts you will have sufficient pastry for the remaining tin.

2 Bake blind at 200°C for 15 minutes. *It is easiest if you place the tarts on a baking tray to cook.*

3 Remove the baking blind material and return the tarts to the oven for a further 3 minutes. Cool in tin.

4 Spread equal amounts of the chocolate over the base of the tarts. Leave until set. Remove the tarts from the tins.

5 Whip the cream until it is slightly thick but can still be poured. Blend the cream, mascarpone and lemon or orange rind together. Sweeten to taste with icing sugar. Spread the cream filling evenly over the chocolate bases and refrigerate while preparing the strawberries.

6 Wipe and dry the strawberries with a cloth, leaving the stalks intact. Put the sugar and water into a saucepan. Stir over a moderate heat until all the sugar has dissolved. Bring to the boil and boil rapidly until the sugar begins to change to a light golden toffee colour. Remove from the heat and stand on a very wet cloth immediately to stop the sugar browning any more.

7 Once the bubbles have subsided, dip the strawberries, holding onto their stalks, into the toffee and place on a greased tray until set. Transfer to the top of the tarts and serve.

Makes 2

Cook's Tip

Any remaining sugar can be spun into angel's hair. Hold two forks together, dip in toffee and then throw over sheets of paper. As it falls the toffee sets. Arrange on top of tarts.

Dried Summer Berries in Wine over Crème Hearts

Dried summer fruits such as strawberries, blueberries and cherries make a simple and delicious topping for this elegant easy-to-make variation of Coeur à la Crème.

150 grams creme fraîche
150 grams quark
½ tsp vanilla essence
1 egg white
3 tblsp caster sugar

Dried Summer Fruits in Wine

3/4 cup dried summer fruits
½ x 375-ml bottle sweet white wine

1 Put the crème fraîche, quark and vanilla essence into a food processor and beat until smooth. Alternatively do this with a beater.

2 In a clean bowl beat the egg white until it is thick and forms stiff peaks.

3 Gradually beat in the caster sugar until the mixture becomes thick and meringue-like (nice and glossy). Arrange the beaten meringue mixture around the top of the cheese in the food processor and pulse to mix in. Do not process on full speed as this will over beat the mixture. Alternatively, fold the egg whites into the beaten cheese mixture.

4 Line 3 baby heart-shaped Coeur à la Crème moulds (see Cook's Tip) with damp muslin cloth and fill with the cheese mixture. Place on a shallow tray and cover with cling wrap. Refrigerate for 8 hours or overnight.

5 To serve, turn out onto a plate and spoon over the berry fruits.

Serves 2

Dried Summer Fruits in Wine

Place the selection of fruits into a saucepan with the wine. Bring to the boil and turn off the heat. Transfer to a non-metallic bowl and stand, covered, for 2-4 hours until the fruits are plump. Serve chilled. I used dried summer fruits – a mix that included dried strawberries, blueberries, cranberries and cherries. If these are not available, use apricots, peaches, mangoes and sultanas.

Cook's Tip

A Coeur à la Crème mould is a heart-shaped mould made from china with holes in the base for the whey to drain away. They are available in 2 sizes, large and small.

Wine Selection

Most sweet dessert wines will fare well here; those with an intense honeyed fruit will be a taste sensation when used in this dish. Our wine suggestion: Try the well-priced Corbans Private Bin Late Harvest Semillon/Sauvignon Blanc.

Chocolate & Kahlua Tiramisu

If you are a fan of tiramisu, then this chocolate version will have you reeling. Chocolate, they say, is the food of love, so make sure you have some on the menu next time you plan a romantic dinner.

¼ cup Kahlua
½ x 125-gram packet sponge finger biscuits
75 grams dark chocolate, melted
2 egg whites

300 grams mascarpone cheese
1 egg yolk
½ cup caster sugar
about ¼ cup grated chocolate for the top

1 Warm the Kahlua. Dip half the sponge finger biscuits in the Kahlua and use to line the base of a 2-cup capacity serving dish. Save the Kahlua as you will need it again.

2 In a food processor put the chocolate, mascarpone cheese and egg yolk and blend together well.

3 In a clean bowl, whip the egg whites until soft peaks form.

4 Gradually whip in the caster sugar until the mixture becomes thick and glossy and meringue-like. Arrange the mixture on top of the mascarpone in the food processor and pulse until it is blended in.

5 Spoon half over the sponge finger biscuits. Dip the remaining biscuits into the remaining Kahlua and place on top. Cover with the remaining chocolate mixture and spread out evenly. Sprinkle over the grated chocolate and refrigerate before serving.

I always prefer to eat Tiramisu on the day it is made.

S e r v e s   2 (*with a little left over for indulgence*)

Sundays in Summer

Sundays in summer are one of my favourite days for entertaining. Saturdays are for organising and sport and shopping; Sundays are for catching up with friends (even better if it is a long weekend). These ideas are to be enjoyed casually on lazy summer days.

Salad Niçoise

1 lettuce
250 grams green beans
8-10 anchovy fillets
400 grams fresh tomatoes,
    sliced

185-gram can tuna,
    drained and flaked
4 hardboiled eggs, sliced
¼-½ cup black olives
1 tblsp capers

Dressing

1 clove garlic, peeled and
    mashed
2 tblsp chopped fresh basil
¼ cup olive oil

2 tblsp white wine vinegar
1 tsp wholegrain mustard
freshly ground black
    pepper

1 Wash lettuce and dry well. Put leaves in dry tea towels and refrigerate for 30 minutes to help to crisp.

2 Top and tail beans, blanch in boiling salted water for 2-3 minutes, drain and refresh in cold water. Drain dry on paper towel.

3 Cut anchovy fillets in half lengthways.

4 Arrange lettuce leaves, whole beans, sliced tomatoes, flaked tuna and hardboiled egg slices in layers on a platter. On top, use halved anchovy fillets to make a lattice pattern, place black olives in the diamonds of the lattice, sprinkle with capers.

5 Just before serving, drizzle over the dressing. Enjoy with warm olive and onion bread.

Serves 4

Dressing

In a screw-top jar, combine garlic, basil, olive oil, white wine vinegar, wholegrain mustard and pepper. Shake well.

Cook's Tip

By crushing a clove of garlic with the blade of a heavy knife, you will break the skin at the base, allowing it to peel away easily. Always keep a garlic board in the kitchen as garlic will taint a wooden board terribly.

Wine Selection

As this dish is fresh and light in texture and flavour, try with a light, crisp Sauvignon. Our wine suggestion: The latest release from Longridge of Hawkes Bay, or the good value Corbans Waimanu.

Fresh Cream, Cheese & Olive Tart

This tart is truly an olive lover's dream. I have made the pastry base, but you could use a pre-made short savoury pastry if you wish.

Tapenade

¾ cup black olives, stoned
50-gram can anchovy
    fillets, drained

1½ tblsp capers
2 tblsp olive oil
1 tblsp lemon juice

Short Pastry

1 cup flour
½ tsp salt
about 3 tblsp cold water

100 grams butter
    (preferably unsalted)

Filling

2 eggs
1 tblsp chopped fresh herbs
    (marjoram, oregano,
    parsley)

1 cup finely grated tasty
    cheese
3 tblsp cream

1 To make the tapenade, in a food processor, combine olives, anchovies and capers, and process until smooth. With the machine still running, gradually pour in olive oil and finally the lemon juice.

2 Sift the pastry flour and salt into a bowl. Cut in the butter until the mixture resembles fine crumbs. Stir in sufficient water to form a stiff dough. Alternatively, make the pastry in a food processor.

3 Turn out and knead lightly. Roll out dough to line the base and sides of a 23-cm loose bottom flan tin.

4 Bake blind at 200°C for 12-15 minutes. Remove the baking blind material and return to the oven for about 3-5 minutes or until the base has dried out.

5 Spread the tapenade over the base of the tart.

6 To make the filling, beat the eggs and cream together, add herbs and mix in grated cheese. Carefully spoon filling evenly over the tapenade.

7 Cook at 180°C for 20-25 minutes, or until the filling is cooked and golden.

8 Serve warm, accompanied by tomatoes in a balsamic vinegar dressing.

Serves 6-8

Wine Selection

Olive flavours dominate this dish; try it matched with a red wine with more fruit than oak. Our wine suggestion: Stoneleigh Vineyard Marlborough Cabernet Sauvignon or Robard & Butler Shiraz.

Turkey & Berry Salad with Blue Cheese & Cranberry Vinaigrette

Fresh berries and blue cheese make a perfect match and complement turkey so well. The turkey portions now found in supermarkets make this once-a-year special meat available all year through. If you do not have turkey, substitute cooked or smoked chicken.

½ French bread stick
¼ cup olive oil or melted butter
mixed greens for 4 (include watercress and baby salad leaves)
200 grams sliced blue cheese

1 punnet blackberries
200-300 grams sliced cold turkey
4 slices bacon, cooked and crumbled
1 bunch fresh asparagus, peeled and blanched

Dressing

1 cup vinaigrette (see page 78)
2 tblsp cranberry sauce
2 tblsp sour cream (optional)

1 Cut the French stick into ½-cm slices. Brush with olive oil and then grill until the bread slices are crisp.

2 On a large platter, arrange crisp green salad leaves. Slice the blue cheese and toss through the salad with the blackberries, turkey, bacon, and asparagus.

3 Pour over the dressing just before serving and toss in slices of crisp French bread.

Serves 4

Dressing

Blend the vinaigrette and cranberry sauce together. Stir in the sour cream if using.

Makes 1¼ cups

Cook's Tip

Salad greens are best when they are crisp and lightly and freshly coated in the dressing. If your greens are a bit limp, then wash them well in cold water. Shake them gently to dry or use a lettuce spinner and then wrap then in a clean tea towel for about 30 minutes and store in the fridge until needed. Dress the salad just before serving.

Wine Selection

With the varied combination of flavours here a wine with a touch of sweetness will be best. Our wine suggestion: Try a medium Riesling, such as the Corbans Estate Marlborough Riesling.

Racks of Lamb with Parsley Almond Crust & Orange Sauce

These racks of lamb are delicious. Ask your butcher to trim them well to save you time and make them look nicer for presentation.

*4 racks of lamb that have
  been well trimmed
  (4-5 cutlets each)*
¼ cup orange juice
¼ cup white wine
black pepper
1 cup chopped parsley
¼ cup sliced almonds

*1 cup soft white
  breadcrumbs*
2 tblsp orange marmalade
½ tsp grated orange rind
2 tblsp melted butter
¼ cup water
1 tsp honey
2 tsp cornflour

1 Combine orange juice, white wine and black pepper. Place in shallow dish and add racks of lamb. Refrigerate and marinate for 1-2 hours.

2 Remove racks from marinade and reserve the marinade for the sauce.

3 Combine parsley, breadcrumbs, almonds, marmalade, the orange rind and butter, and mix well. Press mixture over meaty part of each rack of lamb.

4 Place the lamb, crumb side up, in baking dish and bake at 200°C for 20-25 minutes or until racks of lamb are cooked as desired. This will give a nice medium lamb. If you want it more well done, cook a further 5-8 minutes.

5 Remove lamb from oven, cover with foil and allow to rest in a warm place 10 minutes before serving with the sauce.

6 To make the sauce, add water or chicken stock, honey and cornflour to reserved marinade. Bring to the boil and simmer for 1 minute until thickened.

Serves 4

Cook's Tip

It is best to use scissors to cut herbs, as much of the flavour will be lost if you chop them on a wooden board.

Wine Selection

Forget the old rule of red wine with red meat and match this dish with a fragrant dry Riesling or an oak aged Sauvignon Blanc to accompany the herbs and citrus flavours. Our wine suggestions: Try the Longridge of Hawkes Bay Oak Aged Sauvignon Blanc or the Stoneleigh Vineyard Marlborough Riesling.

Summer Chilled Cherries

As much as I love cherry pie, I still prefer cherries fresh or very simply prepared. In this recipe they are poached and served well chilled, with whipped cream that has been flavoured with amaretti biscuits. Or you could serve them with chilled yoghurt.

750 grams red cherries
½ cup sugar
¾ cup water
1 tblsp kirsch
70 grams packet blanched almonds, toasted

Amaretti Cream

1 bottle (300 ml) cream
6 amaretti biscuits
a little icing sugar to sweeten

1 Wash and de-stem the cherries. Place in a large frying pan and sprinkle over the sugar and water.

2 Simmer, stirring, over a moderate heat for about 10 minutes until the cherries have softened but have not gone mushy. Stir in the Kirsch.

3 Transfer to a container, cover and chill.

4 To serve, divide the cherries and juice between 6 bowls and toss through equal amounts of the golden toasted almonds.

Spoon over a dollop of Amaretti Cream and serve garnished with fresh mint.

Serves 6

Amaretti Cream

Whip the cream until it forms soft peaks. Crush the amaretti biscuits to fine crumbs and fold through. Sweeten the cream with icing sugar if you wish.

Roast Chicken with Lavender & Basil

Lavender, I hear you say, on chicken? In Provence in the south of France, a herb mixture including lavender, basil, thyme, marjoram and fennel seeds is used to season chicken and fish. Try it – you'll be surprised.

¼ tsp each fennel seeds and black pepper
1 tblsp each chopped fresh basil, thyme and marjoram
1 fresh chicken
2-3 tblsp good olive oil
1 tsp crushed lavender heads (fresh from the garden)
1 tblsp softened butter
1 tblsp flour
1 cup white wine

1 Blend together the fennel seeds, black pepper, fresh basil, thyme, marjoram and lavender.

2 Take the chicken and, using a pair of scissors or a sharp knife, cut out the back bone. Flatten the chicken out by pressing down on the breast bone and tuck the wings underneath.

3 Lift the skin gently from the breast of the chicken and sprinkle half the herbs between the skin and meat.

4 Heat the oil in a cast-iron or ovenproof skillet. Place the chicken skin-side down and brown for about 5 minutes over a moderate heat. Turn the chicken over and spread over the butter.

5 Sprinkle over the remaining herbs and sift the flour. Pour in the wine and bring to the boil.

6 Transfer to a 190°C oven and bake for about 45-60 minutes until cooked. *To test if the chicken is cooked, use a skewer and pierce the chicken through to the bone. The juice should be clear.*

Serves 4

Serve the chicken from the table on a large platter with roasted red and yellow peppers and kumara, and summer green beans tossed in a little garlic butter or flavoured olive oil.

Wine Selection

A subtle blend of complementary herbs infuses masses of flavour into this family chicken dish. A hearty Chardonnay with ripe tropical fruit flavours will best suit this dish of Provence. Our wine suggestion: Corbans Private Bin Chardonnay or Cooks Winemakers Reserve Chardonnay.

Caramel Oranges with Lemon Tuile Biscuits

In place of brandy you could use rum. If you don't have the time to make the tuile biscuits, use macaroons or sponge finger biscuits (savoiardi).

4-6 smallish oranges   *¼ cup brandy*
½ cup sugar   *½ cup orange juice*
¼ cup water

1 Thinly peel the rind from 1 orange and shred finely. Peel the remaining oranges thickly with a knife, removing every trace of the white pith as this is quite bitter. Cut into thin slices and place orange slices and shredded rind in a small heatproof dish.

2 Put the sugar and water into a saucepan and bring to the boil, stirring until the sugar dissolves. Continue boiling until the sugar turns a light golden colour.

3 Lower the heat and carefully add the brandy and orange juice. *It will splutter, so keep your arm well covered in case it spits at you.*

4 Simmer until the toffee dissolves. Remove from heat and allow to cool for 5 minutes before pouring over the oranges. Cover and leave to marinate for at least 2 hours before serving chilled.

5 Serve with Lemon Tuile Biscuits and lashings of whipped cream or yoghurt.

Serves 4

Lemon Tuile Biscuits

These biscuits are crisp and delicate, ideal company for a whole range of desserts or to enjoy with coffee. They keep well in an airtight container.

75 grams softened butter   *1 tsp grated lemon rind*
½ cup caster sugar   *2½ tblsp lemon juice*
½ cup flour, sifted

1 Beat the butter with a wooden spoon until it is creamed in colour. Work in the sugar until it is dissolved.

2 Fold in the flour with the lemon rind and juice. Place teaspoonfuls onto a greased baking tray and spread out with a warm spatula to 5-6 cm in diameter.

3 Bake at 200°C for 4-5 minutes or until the outer rim turns a biscuit colour.

4 Remove from the tray and cool for a few seconds before carefully placing the biscuits over a rolling pin. Leave for 1-2 minutes until the shape is set. Alternatively, roll around the handle of a wooden spoon into a cigarette shape, or leave as they are – it's up to you.

Makes 20

Barbecue in Style

Barbecues are so much a part of the way we live, I cannot imagine a summer entertaining without them. Everyone can be involved, even the kids. I have to admit to keeping a watchful eye on Warwick and good friend Dave on the cooking. For some reason after not even attempting a grilled chop through the winter, they seem to think that they have all the qualifications for taking over at the barbecue! If it's the same in your house then let them go, but try to keep the fork out of their hands or the meat will end up like a sieve!

Spicy Salmon

Just delicious. I created this recipe following a trip to Tabasco in Louisiana for *Next*.

½ tsp each dried basil, thyme and ground black pepper

2 tblsp finely chopped parsley

4 sun-dried red tomatoes in oil, finely diced

2 tsp Tabasco sauce

2 tblsp smooth tomato sauce (such as Watties) or purée

juice of ½ lemon

1 spring onion, finely chopped

1 kg whole side of fresh salmon

1 In a bowl mix together the dried herbs and pepper, parsley, sun-dried tomatoes, Tabasco and tomato sauces, lemon juice and spring onion.

2 Rub this mixture all over the salmon flesh. Place in a large dish or on a plate and set aside for 1 hour before cooking.

3 Heat the barbecue to moderately hot and brush liberally with good olive oil. Place the salmon, topping side down, onto the hot plate and cook for 7 minutes. Turn and cook the other side for 7-8 minutes until the salmon is still a little pink on the inside. *You can see this by looking at the end of the salmon or just parting the flesh a little bit.*

4 Serve the salmon hot with a little extra olive oil or butter on top.

To cook in foil, wrap the salmon in foil and cook on the barbecue at the same heat and time. Check before serving. Cooking time will vary depending on the thickness of the salmon. Do not overcook, as it is much better a fraction underdone.

Serves 6-8

Wine Selection

Warm, spicy herbal flavours are infused into the salmon, and a touch of sweetness is provided by the crispy topping. Match with a crisp, dry Riesling with plenty of spicy fruit. Our wine suggestion: The well-known Corbans Private Bin Amberley Rielsing.

Fillet of Beef with Anchovies

Make sure you get a middle piece of the fillet, as the eye end or thicker end will need too long on the barbecue before it is cooked.

56-gram tin anchovies,
 well drained

2 tblsp chopped sun-dried
 red peppers

1 tblsp sun-dried tomato
 paste (see page 26)

1 cup red wine

lashings freshly ground
 black pepper

¼ cup chopped fresh
 oregano

750 gram piece eye fillet

1 tblsp olive oil

1 Chop the anchovies well and mix in a bowl with the sun-dried red peppers, sun-dried tomato paste, black pepper and oregano.

2 Using a sharp long knife, make a cut through the centre of the eye fillet. If possible, do not pierce all the way through to the other end. Carefully stuff the filling into the cut and secure the cut end with a skewer.

3 Transfer the beef to a non-metallic dish and pour over the red wine and oil. Cover and leave to marinate for about 4 hours if possible. Turn occasionally.

4 Heat the barbecue to very hot and brush generously with olive oil. Add the beef and seal on all sides over a high heat. Then turn down the heat to medium and continue to cook the beef, turning occasionally, for about 40 minutes.

5 Stand for 5 minutes before carving.

6 Serve sliced hot or cold later on.

Serves 6

Wine Selection

Choose a young, bold red wine with plenty of ripe fruit and a touch of tannin to complement the rareness of the beef. Our wine suggestions: Corbans Private Bin Hawkes Bay Cabernet Sauvignon or the well-priced Robard & Butler Shiraz.

Cardamom Snaps with Fresh Strawberries & Cream

I have left these cardamom-scented snaps flat and layered them with cream and strawberries.

125 grams butter
½ cup sugar
¼ cup golden syrup
¾ cup flour
1 tsp cardamom

1 Put the butter, sugar and golden syrup in a saucepan and heat slowly until the butter has melted. Do not boil the liquid as it will evaporate.

2 Sift the flour and cardamom together and stir into the mixture.

3 Place teaspoonfuls of the mixture onto a greased baking sheet.

4 Bake at 180°C for 5-7 minutes, or until the snaps are golden and formed into their lacework pattern.

5 Cool on the sheets for a minute before lifting onto a cake rack to cool. *If the snaps harden on the tray, return to the oven for a minute to soften.*

Serves 4

To serve, hull a punnet of strawberries sweetened with icing sugar. Whip a 300 ml bottle of cream and layer the cardamom snaps with the cream and strawberries. You can also serve with a strawberry sauce made by puréeing about ½ a punnet of strawberries with a little icing sugar.

Wine Selection

It's summer, so enjoy something special with these wonderfully perfumed strawberries. Our wine suggestion: Amadeus Méthode Champenoise or Champernay Méthode Champenoise.

Lemon Fudge Slice

If you like lemon honey you will love this one.

1 ¼ cups flour
125 grams butter
2 tblsp sugar

Filling

150 grams butter, melted
½ cup lemon juice
grated rind 2 lemons

5 eggs
½ cup caster sugar
icing sugar to dust with

1 Put the flour, butter and sugar into a food processor and process until the mixture resembles coarse crumbs. This can also be done by hand, by rubbing the butter into the dry ingredients.

2 Press the mixture into the base of a lined 24 cm cake tin. Bake at 180°C for 30 minutes until golden.

3 Beat the butter, lemon juice, lemon rind, eggs, and caster sugar together well.

4 Pour the filling over the base and return to a 160°C oven for 25-30 minutes or until the filling has set. Cool to serve.

5 Dust with icing sugar to serve and serve with fresh fruits and cream.

Serves 8

Lamb Rump with Fresh Herbs

The simplest of marinades is often all that is needed to enhance a beautiful piece of meat. Here fresh rosemary and oregano are blended with a fruity virgin olive oil to really enhance the lamb.

2 sprigs fresh rosemary
2 tblsp chopped fresh oregano
4 tblsp virgin olive oil
juice of 1 lemon
½ tsp finely ground black pepper
½ tsp sea salt
4 lamb rumps

1 Remove the leaves from the branches of rosemary and chop the rosemary and oregano finely. Mix together with the olive oil, lemon juice, black pepper, and salt.

2 Place the well trimmed lamb rumps in a shallow container. Pour over and rub in marinade. Cover and refrigerate for about 2 hours.

3 Heat the barbecue to medium hot and brush well with olive oil. Sear the lamb rumps on all sides and then allow to cook for about 15 minutes turning occasionally. This will give medium rare lamb, but much will depend on the heat of the barbecue and the thickness of the lamb rumps. Make sure that it is not overcooked. Serve sliced.

Serve 6

Wine Selection

Don't overpower the delicate flavours of this dish, a subtle red wine with herbal or minty flavours will be best. Our wine suggestion: Stoneleigh Vineyard Marlborough Cabernet Sauvignon.

Lemon Tarragon Prawns

Lemon infused olive oil, fresh tarragon and ginger give a fresh aniseed flavour to the prawns.

4 tblsp lemon infused olive oil
4 tblsp dry white wine or lemon juice
½ tsp each ground ginger and ground black pepper
3 tblsp chopped fresh tarragon
20 large prawns in their shells
extra lemon infused olive oil for drizzling (optional)

1 In a bowl blend together the oil, white wine or lemon juice, ginger, pepper, and tarragon.

2 Run a rolling pin over the prawns to crush their shells a little. Arrange in a single layer in a shallow dish and pour over the marinade. Cover and marinate for 1-2 hours.

3 Heat the barbecue until it is very hot. Brush well with olive oil. Place the prawns on the barbecue and cook over a high heat for about 6-8 minutes until they are cooked. This time will vary depending on the thickness of the prawns. Serve drizzled with lemon infused olive oil.

Serves 4

Cook's Tip

Colonna lemon infused olive oil is a fabulous product to have on hand for special occasions. If you do not have it, add the grated rind of 1 lemon to the olive oil.

Wine Selection

Lemon, herbs and ginger give these prawns a real flavour boost. They will go best with a Riesling that isn't too young and fresh. Our wine suggestion: Try the soft, mellow style of the Corbans Private Bin Amberley Riesling.

Pork Fillets with Green Peppercorns

Green peppercorns were a new trend food way back in the 80s. The unripened pepper berries in brine are fragrant and spicy and ideal with pork.

1 tblsp green peppercorns,
    well drained and
    chopped
2 cloves garlic, peeled and
    crushed
2 tsp grated lemon rind

½ cup lemon juice
good grinding of freshly
    ground black pepper
1 tblsp honey
500 grams pork fillets

Sauce

reserved marinade
½ cup white wine
½ cup cream

1 Combine the peppercorns, garlic, lemon rind, lemon juice, pepper and honey in a bowl. Place the fillets of pork in a shallow lidded container and pour over the marinade, tossing well to coat evenly.

2 Cover and refrigerate for at least 2 hours.

3 Heat the barbecue until it is quite hot and brush well with olive oil. Remove the pork from the marinade, reserving the marinade. Place the pork fillets on the barbecue and cook, turning once seared, for 8-10 minutes until tender.

4 Place the reserved marinade in a saucepan and bring to the boil with the white wine and cream. Allow to reduce by one-third.

5 Serve the pork sliced, with the sauce to accompany.

Serves 4

Wine Selection

Spicy lemon flavours abound in this dish. Match them with a rich, full flavoured Riesling. Our wine suggestion: Corbans Private Bin Amberley Riesling.

Barbecue Tips

- Do not put lots of oil on the barbecue plate, just enough to prevent the food from sticking. Otherwise you will partially deep fry the food.

- Have the barbecue hot, or the food will stew when it goes on. You need to seal the meat on both sides first and for this you need a hot barbecue.

- Throw away barbecue forks. They turn good food into sieves. Use tongs and metal spatula.

- Sweet marinades will burn, so be careful with the amounts of sugar, honey and sweet sauces that you use.

- You do not need so much marinade that the food swims in it. It's a waste of good ingredients. Use enough to give good flavour and coat the meat, poultry or fish.

- When putting marinades together, do not have too many competing flavours or the meat will suffer. Keep it simple.

- Always clean the barbecue well before and after cooking.

Salad Leaves

Salads do not have to be made of just one kind of lettuce for they come red, green, spiky, bitter, hot, and sweet, and add such great taste. Here's a quick rundown on some of the leaves that are most commonly available.

Raddichio: this is actually a red-leafed Italian member of the chicory family but is more often used as a salad green. It has deep burgundy leaves with white veins, which have a slightly bitter flavour and firm but tender leaves. Choose leaves that are full of colour with no signs of browning.

Curly Endive (Frisée): this grows in loose heads of lacy green rimmed lettuce that curl at the tips. It has a mildly bitter flavour and is quite astringent, ideal for incorporating into a salad with other better known salad leaves.

Cos: this is an old-fashioned winter lettuce, often known as Romaine. It has an elongated head with coarse leaves that are crunchy and can be slightly astringent. Used in a Caesar salad.

Butterhead or Buttercrunch: this lettuce has a soft texture with a flat smooth leaf, which sometimes has a greasy or buttery feel to it. Some of these varieties have heart-shaped leaves whereas others are more rounded. It is ideal for summer salads.

Rocket: a hot peppery salad leaf with deep mid-green leaves. It is also called Arugula. It is ideal to add to a salad; the nicest leaves are the young tender shoots.

Sorrel: occasionally you will find this rather old-fashioned leaf. It has a lemony flavour and the torn leaves add a nice sharp contrast to any salad.

Lollo Rosso or Lollo Biondo: soft frilly leaves, which add texture and colour.

Red Oak Leaf: soft red leaves, which add great colour and a light sharp flavour.

Basic Salad Dressings

These classic dressings need good quality ingredients: good olive oil, to avoid an oily bland taste, and wine vinegar, not white vinegar which will take your breath away. While I promote the use of prepared foods of acceptable quality, bought dressings don't fit into this category – they are tasteless. As for the low calorie dressings, I would not waste my money. Use a drop of Balsamic vinegar or fresh lemon juice instead.

Vinaigrette

Use 3 parts olive oil to 1 part white wine vinegar. Season well with salt, pepper and a dash of prepared mustard. It is that easy. You can make variations but this easy recipe is often the best for a complex salad with a number of flavours. Too many flavours in a salad can be totally detrimental to the whole dish.

It is your choice whether you make the dressing in a jar and shake (of course with the lid on), blend it in a jug or process it until thick.

Variations

- *Herb:* Add chopped fresh herbs and alter the level of mustard.

- *Garlic:* Add 1 small clove crushed garlic and allow to stand for 30 minutes before using.

- *Balsamic:* Use a combination of white wine and balsamic vinegar (especially nice with tomato and bocconcini and a basil salad).

- *Lemon Olive Oil:* Remove 2 tablespoonfuls of the olive oil and replace with lemon infused olive oil.

- *Cream:* Add 2 tblsp sour cream and blend well.

- *Blue Cheese:* Blend 2-3 tblsp blue cheese into the vinaigrette.

Mayonnaise

My first introduction to mayonnaise came by way of a can of condensed milk at about age 8. Terrible stuff, even worse if made with malt vinegar. Nor do I like bottled mayonnaise, though I do admit to having it on standby should ever I be caught out. Why go to all the trouble of making a delicious salad with the very best of summer's ingredients, only to spoil it with a less than delicious bought mayonnaise?

2 egg yolks
squeeze lemon juice
2 tblsp tarragon vinegar or white wine vinegar
1 tsp Dijon Mustard
1 cup olive oil
salt and white pepper

1 Beat the egg yolks, lemon juice, vinegar and mustard well with a wooden spoon or in a food processor.

2 Gradually (use a whisk now if making by hand) blend in half the olive oil, drop by drop, so the egg yolks can absorb the oil.

3 Continue in this fashion, only adding the oil a little faster, until all the oil has been used. The mayonnaise should be thick. *Should the mayonnaise separate on you, do not panic. In a clean bowl beat another egg yolk. Then gradually blend in the separated mixture bit by bit. This happens if the oil has been added too fast.*

4 Season the mayonnaise with salt and white pepper. Black pepper will make it look like the flies have walked all over it.

Variations

- **Aioli:** Add 2-3 crushed cloves garlic to the mayonnaise (or more if you are a garlic freak). Nice as a dip with crudités.

- **Tartare:** Bad versions are available everywhere. Add 1 tblsp each of chopped tarragon and chives. Blend in 2 tblsp chopped gherkins and capers. Stand 1 hour before serving.

- **Aillade:** Add crushed garlic and chopped walnuts, about ¼-½ cup crushed walnuts.

- **Remoulade:** Add 2 tblsp each chopped capers and gherkins and 2 finely chopped anchovy fillets. Season with a tsp each of chopped parsley, tarragon and chervil. Stand 1 hour before serving. This is lovely with chicken and fish.

- **Thousand Island:** This is not supposed to be a smooth pink coloured dressing. To the basic mix add 2 tblsp each chopped stuffed olives and green pepper, 1 hardboiled egg (diced), 1 tblsp each minced onion, parsley and tomato purée.

- **Mustard:** Add 1 tblsp wholeseed mustard.

Tips For Great Salads

- Use only the freshest and best ingredients for a salad.

- Use the best dressings and only a light covering. Toss as you serve, as the oil and vinegar clog the pores of the leaves and the leaves begin to wilt.

- Use a selection of leaves: include something for bulk such as a buttercrunch; add something for a hotter or spicier flavour, like watercress or rocket; then colour by way of herbs or flowers; and that's it. Crisp and fresh.

- Use a salad spinner to ensure that all the water is removed from the leaves. Or wash the leaves in cold water, shake carefully and wrap in a clean tea towel. Shake well and refrigerate for 30 minutes to crisp.

- Do not make salads in advance. Once washed and well drained of water, the leaves will keep crisp in a fridge for about 3 hours. After that they will begin to wilt.

Warming Up Winter

I love the sound of rain crashing on the roof and the delicious smells of winter casseroles. In winter we hibernate from many things, but not entertaining. Winter foods can be so easy to prepare and the cooler weather increases hearty appetites.

Tuscan Chicken with Grilled Polenta

This well-flavoured chicken dish is from Catherine Bell of Auckland's Epicurean Workshop and appeared in *Next* a year or so back.

8 large chicken pieces	2 tsp fresh rosemary leaves
3 stalks celery, finely sliced	or 1 tsp dried
6 shallots, peeled and	1 tsp salt
quartered, or 1 onion,	freshly ground black
diced	pepper
15 black olives, pitted	2 tblsp olive oil
½ cup sultanas or raisins	¾ cup beef stock
¼ cup capers	¼ cup tomato paste
¾ cup dry red wine	extra sage leaves for
1 tblsp chopped fresh sage	garnish
or 1 tsp dried	

1 Trim any excess fat from the chicken and cut the chicken pieces.

2 In a large lidded non-metallic container put the chicken, celery, shallots, olives, sultanas and capers. Add the dry red wine and sprinkle over the sage, rosemary, salt, and good grindings of black pepper. Mix thoroughly. Cover and refrigerate for 8 hours or overnight.

3 Heat the olive oil in an ovenproof frying pan. Lift the chicken from the marinade and reserve the marinade. Sauté over a moderate heat until the chicken is golden all over.

4 Mix the stock and tomato paste together and add to the marinade. When all the chicken pieces are golden brown, pour the marinade mixture over the chicken and bring to a simmer.

5 Transfer the frying pan to the oven and cook at 180°C for 30-40 minutes until the chicken is tender. Baste 3-4 times during the cooking. Serve the chicken with grilled polenta.

Serves 4

Grilled Polenta

Polenta is peasant food from Italy. Add extra flavouring such as grated Parmesan cheese or freshly chopped herbs. Garnish with plenty of butter before grilling.

5 cups light chicken stock	1¾ cups instant polenta
2 tsp salt	50 grams unsalted butter

1 Bring the chicken stock and the salt to the boil in a large saucepan. Gradually pour in the polenta, whisking as you add it to avoid lumps.

2 Using a wooden spoon, stir the thickened mixture for about 5 minutes.

3 Add the butter and stir in.

4 Spread the mixture onto a greased tray to about 5 cm thickness. Set aside and allow the mixture to cool. When cool, cut the polenta into wedges or diamond shapes. Brush the pieces with melted butter or olive oil and grill on both sides until golden.

S e r v e s 4

C o o k ' s T i p

If using regular polenta, cooking time is 35 minutes, stirring all the time over low heat until the polenta leaves the sides of the pot.

Dried Fruits with Lemon Tea & Palmiers

Dried fruits soaked in citrus lemon tea and dessert wine are wonderful served slightly warm with crispy Palmiers and dollops of cream for an easy winter dessert.

3 cups boiling water
3 lemon scented tea bags
½ cup dessert wine
½ cup sugar

100 grams each of the
following dried fruits:
raisins, mangoes,
apricots, apples, and figs

Palmiers

1 pre-rolled puff pastry sheet
milk to glaze
about 6 tsp caster sugar

1 Pour the boiling water over the tea bags and allow them to steep for about 5 minutes. Strain the water into a saucepan. Add the dessert wine and sugar. Bring to the boil and simmer, stirring until the sugar has dissolved.

2 Add the dried fruits and allow to poach gently for 10 minutes.

3 Remove the fruit from the heat and transfer the fruit to a lidded container.

4 Boil the juice until it has reduced by a quarter. Pour back over the fruit. Cover and chill.

5 To serve, warm the fruit and syrup through and serve in bowls with a Palmier and cream.

Serves 6

Palmiers

1 Place 1 sheet of pastry on a lightly floured board and brush with milk.

2 Sprinkle about 2 tsp sugar over the pastry sheet. Fold the outer two edges to the centre without them actually touching. Brush each side with milk and sprinkle with a further 2 tsp sugar. Fold the outer edges in again to the centre. Then carefully fold together, pressing firmly. Use a sharp knife to cut the pastry length at 0.5 cm widths and place these on a greased baking tray.

3 Press down with a rolling pin to slightly flatten each Palmier. Brush with milk and sprinkle the remaining caster sugar on top.

4 Bake at 190°C fan bake, or 210°C for about 12-15 minutes until the heart-shaped Palmiers are crispy and golden.

Store in an airtight container.

Makes 20

Lamb Shank Tagine

Lamb shanks have recently made a re-entry in the popular food stakes. They're full of flavour, very reasonable in price and usually thoroughly enjoyed by everyone. Try these with couscous or bowls of steaming mashed potatoes.

½ cup sultanas

½ cup sherry (preferably dry)

2 tblsp oil

6 lamb shanks

2 large onions, peeled and chopped finely

4 cloves garlic, peeled and mashed

5 cm piece fresh ginger, peeled and grated

2 tsp ground coriander

2 cups chicken or vegetable stock

6-8 strands saffron or 1-2 tsp turmeric

1 cinnamon stick (or ½ tsp ground cinnamon)

1 lemon

2 tsp salt

pepper

1 Soak sultanas in sherry for about 30 minutes. Heat oil in a large lidded frying pan and brown lamb shanks well on all sides. Add onions, garlic, ginger, and coriander and cook 2 minutes.

2 Heat stock and add saffron. Stand for 2 minutes. (If using turmeric, there is no need to allow the stock and turmeric to infuse.)

3 Add sultanas and sherry, cinnamon stick and saffron stock to the pan and bring to boil. Reduce heat, cover and simmer for 1-1¼ hours until the lamb shanks are tender.

4 Finely slice the lemon and sprinkle with salt. Cover with boiling water and set aside until lamb shanks are cooked, then drain.

5 When the shanks are cooked, discard cinnamon stick. Purée half the sauce in a blender or food processor. Return the purée to shanks and add lemon slices. Season with pepper. Serve hot.

6 Try serving with couscous and broccoli tossed in ginger and butter.

S e r v e s   4 - 6

W i n e   S e l e c t i o n

Warm, rich and spicy; this dish needs a wine with power and flavour. Our wine suggestion: A soft, oaky Robard & Butler Cabernet Shiraz.

Pear & Lemon Cream Pie

This wonderful dessert – crisp, buttery pastry and a light layer of pears in a creamy sauce – has to be tried to be believed!

2½ cups flour	*225 grams unsalted butter*
2 tsp baking powder	*2 egg yolks*
½ cup fine semolina	*little water*
¾ cup icing sugar	

Filling

grated rind 2 lemons	*6 medium ripe pears,*
¾ cup sour cream	*peeled, cored, and*
½ cup caster sugar	*thinly sliced*
2 eggs	

1 Put the flour, baking powder, semolina, icing sugar and chilled diced butter into a food processor and process until the mixture resembles crumbs. *The butter should be well chilled; a room temperature butter will make a greasy pastry that will end up tough and dry.*

2 Mix the egg yolks with about 2 tblsp water and pulse in until the mixture forms small moist balls of dough. Add more water if necessary.

3 Turn out onto a board and bring together to form a ball. Roll two-thirds out to cover the base and sides of a 24-cm loose bottomed flan.

Place in the refrigerator with remaining pastry while preparing the filling.

4 In a bowl beat together the lemon rind, sour cream, sugar, and eggs. Toss the prepared pears in the mixture. Pour the filling into the prepared flan.

5 Roll out the remaining pastry and cover the flan, sealing the edges together well. Decorate with any pastry scraps. Bake at 220°C for 10 minutes and then lower the temperature to 180°C for another 35-40 minutes until the pastry is golden and the pears are cooked.

Serve warm or cold.

Cook's Tip

Semolina is coarsely ground flour. It will add a delicious crunchy texture to this pastry. You do not have to use semolina but you will need to add something else in its place, such as flour or cornflour. If you do not have time to make the pastry, use 2 x 400 gram packets of buttercrust pastry.

Wine Selection

The citrus flavours of the pie predominate and need a floral and fruity wine style, such as a medium Riesling. Our wine suggestion: Stoneleigh Vineyard Marlborough Rhine Riesling or try the Corbans Estate Marlborough Gewurztraminer.

Venison Sausages in Red Wine

A hearty casserole made from tasty venison sausages would be a great hit at a casual evening in front of a roaring fire. It's an adaption of a more sophisticated beef in red wine.

8 thick venison sausages

2 tblsp clarified butter or
    olive oil

4 rashers bacon, trimmed
    and diced

8 baby onions, peeled and
    halved

1 tblsp flour

2 cloves garlic, peeled and
    crushed

350 grams button
    mushrooms

1½ cups red wine

1 bouquet garni

salt and pepper

1 Grill the sausages under a medium heat until golden brown. Spilt in half lengthwise or cut into thick pieces.

2 Heat the butter or olive oil in a ovenproof casserole and cook the bacon and onions over a moderately high heat for about 5 minutes until the onions have softened and begun to colour lightly.

3 Lower the heat. Add the garlic and mushrooms and cook tossing the mushrooms for about a further 2 minutes until it all smells wonderfully fragrant.

4 Sprinkle in the flour and shake or stir until all the white speaks have gone. *If any white flour particles remain, these will lump when you add liquid.*

5 Stir in the red wine and bring to the boil. Add the bouquet garni and season well with salt and pepper. Cover and simmer on top of the stove or in a 180°C oven for about 40-45 minutes until cooked. Remove the bouquet garni before serving.

6 Serve hot with a big bowl of mashed potatoes or freshly cooked pasta.

Serves 4

Wine Selection

A Cabernet/Merlot that's not too oaky will be great both in the casserole and to drink with the meal. Our wine suggestion: Longridge of Hawkes Bay Cabernet/Merlot.

Peach & Pecan Upsidedown Cake

Use canned peaches in winter and serve with a good pouring of custard. This old-fashioned favourite will win rave reviews.

25 grams softened butter
¼ cup brown sugar
6 peach halves, canned
70-gram packet dessert
  pecans
¾ cup caster sugar

100 grams butter
1 egg
1 tsp vanilla essence
1¼ cups flour
2 tsp baking powder
½ cup milk

1 Cream first measure of butter and brown sugar together and spread thickly over base of 23-cm round loose bottom cake tin.

2 Arrange peach halves and pecans attractively on the creamed sugar. Chop any unused pecans and fold them into the cake mixture.

3 Cream second measure of sugar and butter until light and fluffy.

4 Beat in the egg and vanilla essence.

5 Carefully fold in sifted flour and baking powder alternately with milk. Spoon the mixture evenly over the peaches.

6 Bake at 180°C for 40-45 minutes or until a skewer inserted comes out clean.

7 Stand on a wire rack for 5 minutes. Invert cake onto serving plate and remove base and sides. Serve hot or warm with pouring cream or custard.

Serves 6-8

Cook's Tip

If using fresh peaches in summer, first blanch them in boiling water for 1-2 minutes then refresh in cold. Peel, halve and stone. You will need 3 large peaches.

Corbans Estate Varietals

Building on a history of quality wines since 1902, Corbans has just released a new range of four single varietal wines which are excellent value for money. There are two wines from Gisborne – a Chardonnay and a Sauvignon Blanc – and two wines from Marlborough – a Riesling and a Gewurztraminer. The wines in this range are of excellent quality, consistent with Corbans' medal-winning heritage. All of the wines in the Corbans Estate range are ideal food wines and great value for everyday.

Robard & Butler Range

Based on the concept of a French wine negociant, Robard & Butler has built a solid reputation for offering good wines at a fair price. Within the range are a number of local and imported wines, including Chardonnay Méthode Champenoise, South East Australian Cabernet

Shiraz and Chardonnay. There is always something new and special in the range to ensure wine-lovers a few surprises!

Longridge of Hawkes Bay Range

A leading boutique winemaker, Longridge of Hawkes Bay offers a range of premium varietal wines from three vineyards – Omaranui, Tuki Tuki and Haumoana – which are situated about ten kilometres south of Napier. The specific geography of the region, with its sheltered valleys and high sunshine hours, produces the superior grapes used in making these premium wines. Longridge of Hawkes Bay offers a range of premium

varietals – Chardonnay, Sauvignon Blanc Oak Aged, Gewurztraminer (a trophy winner for the best wine in that style at a recent national wine awards) and Cabernet Sauvignon.

Stoneleigh Vineyard Marlborough Range

Situated on the plains of the Wairau River in Marlborough, the Stoneleigh Vineyard derives its name from the 'stony paddocks' of the region. The river plains, with their free-draining stony soils and layers of moisture-retaining silt, contribute to the

exceptional quality of Stoneleigh wines. Since they were launched in 1986, Stoneleigh wines have had outstanding medal successes in both international and domestic wine competitions. More than 100 medals – including 15 gold medals – have been won. The Stoneleigh range includes Sauvignon Blanc, Chardonnay, Rhine Riesling and Cabernet Sauvignon.

Corbans Private Bin Range

Corbans Private Bin is a range of flagship premium varietals selected from New Zealand's premier wine-growing regions. Each wine is chosen as an excellent example of the wine styles that prosper within those regions. For example, Chardonnays from Gisborne and Marlborough, Rhine Riesling from Amberley, Sauvignon Blanc from Marlborough

and Cabernet Sauvignon from Hawkes Bay. The Corbans Private Bin range has a strong heritage of medal success, including New Zealand's ultimate accolade for outstanding quality – the champion wine of the show at the national wine awards. Wine-lovers recognise this range for its quality.

Corbans Amadeus Méthode Champenoise

Amadeus is a premium New Zealand Méthode Champenoise. It is made from a blend of Pinot Noir and Chardonnay grapes grown in Hawkes Bay. The wine is bottle-fermented, with each bottle handturned in the traditional manner of Champagne-style wines. With the benefit of three years of bottle ageing, Amadeus has a light and elegant, crisp yeasty nose and fine bead. It has achieved significant medal success and is an excellent example of this wine style.

Cooks Winemakers Reserve Range

The Cooks Winemakers Reserve range features premium varietals which have been sourced historically

from Hawkes Bay. The Chardonnay is perhaps the most famous wine from the range, with a strong history of gold medal success dating back to the early 1980s.

Index